Atlas of the European novel

1800–1900

Atlas of the European novel

1800–1900

Franco Moretti

V

VERSO

London • New York

First published by Verso 1998
© Franco Moretti 1998
Paperback edition first published by Verso 1999
© Franco Moretti 1999
First published as *Atlante del romanzo europeo 1800–1900*
© Giulio Einaudi editore spa, Turin, 1997

Reprinted in 2007, 2009 , 2011 , 2015

Verso
UK: 6 Meard Street, London W1V 3HR
US: 20 Jay Street, Suite 1010, Brooklyn, NY 11201

Verso is the imprint of New Left Books
ISBN 1-85984-224-0
ISBN 978-1-85984-224-9

British Library Cataloguing in Publication Data
A catalogue record for this book is available from the British Library

Library of Congress Cataloging-in-Publication Data
A catalog record for this book is available from the Library of Congress

Designed and typeset by
The Running Head Limited, London and Cambridge
Printed by Maple Press

Contents

List of figures

Acknowledgements

The following translations have been used (and, where necessary, modified): Honoré de Balzac, *Old Goriot* (Marion Ayton Crawfor, Penguin Books, 1951); *Lost Illusions* (Herbert J. Hunt, Penguin Books, 1971); *Cousin Bette* (Marion Ayton Crawfor, Penguin Books, 1965); *A Harlot High and Low* (Rayner Heppenstall, Penguin Books, 1970); Gustave Flaubert, *Sentimental Education* (Douglas Parmée, Oxford University Press, 1989).

Introduction
Towards a geography of literature

See, my son,
time here turns into space

RICHARD WAGNER, *Parsifal*

1. *'General, you make use of maps...'*

An atlas of the novel. Behind these words, lies a very simple idea: that geography is not an inert container, is not a box where cultural history 'happens', but an active force, that pervades the literary field and shapes it in depth. Making the connection between geography and literature explicit, then – mapping it: because a map is precisely that, a connection made visible – will allow us to see some significant relationships that have so far escaped us.

Such a literary geography, however, can refer to two very different things. It may indicate the study *of space in literature*; or else, *of literature in space*. In the first case, the dominant is a fictional one: Balzac's *version* of Paris, the Africa of colonial romances, Austen's redrawing of Britain. In the second case, it is real historical space: provincial libraries of Victorian Britain, or the European diffusion of *Don Quixote* and *Buddenbrooks*. The two spaces may occasionally (and interestingly) overlap, but they are essentially different, and I will treat them as such: fictional space in the first two chapters of the book, and historical space in the third one.

Still, the distinction between the two spaces does not affect the research method, which is the same everywhere, and is based on the systematic use of maps. Of maps, I mean, not as metaphors, and even less as ornaments of discourse, but as analytical tools: that dissect the text in an unusual way, bringing to light relations that would otherwise remain hidden. A good map is worth a thousand words, cartographers say, and they are right: because it *produces* a thousand words:

it raises doubts, ideas. It poses new questions, and forces you to look for new answers.

Maps, then, as intellectual tools. But in what sense? Thus Charles Sanders Peirce, in 1906:

> Come on, my Reader, and let us construct a diagram to illustrate the general course of thought; I mean a System of diagrammatization by means of which any course of thought can be represented with exactitude. 'But why do that, when the thought itself is present to us?' Such, substantially, has been the interrogative objection raised by more than one or two superior intelligences, among whom I single out an eminent and glorious General.
>
> Recluse that I am, I was not ready with the counter-question, which should have run, 'General, you make use of maps during a campaign, I believe. But why should you do so, when the country they represent is right there?'

And after a brilliant exchange where the eminent General is thoroughly routed, here are Peirce's conclusions:

> Well, General [. . .], if I may try to state the matter after you, one can make exact experiments upon uniform diagrams; and when one does so, one must keep a bright lookout for unintended and unexpected changes thereby brought about in the relations of different significant parts of the diagram to one another. Such operations upon diagrams, whether external or imaginary, take the place of the experiments upon real things that one performs in chemical and physical research. Chemists have ere now, I need not say, described experimentation as the putting of questions to Nature. Just so, experiments upon diagrams are questions put to the Nature of the relations concerned.[1]

Questions put to the form of the novel, and its internal relations: this is what my maps try to do. And they really often felt like so many experiments: some easier, some harder, and all of them teeming with variables that I kept changing and changing (which characters should I map? which narrative moments? which elements of the context?) until I felt I had found a good answer. An answer, an image – a *pattern* that made me see a book, or a genre, in a fresh and interesting way: and whose clarity, I soon realized, was directly proportional to the simplicity and abundance of the data on which it was based. The

[1] 'Prolegomena to an Apology for Pragmaticism', *The Monist*, 16, January 1906, pp. 492–3.

'experiment' succeeded, in other words, thanks to abstraction and quantification: consistent, wide series, where the final significance of a form was always greater than the sum of the separate texts. It's one of the frontiers of critical work: the challenge of quantity – of the 99 percent of all published literature that disappears from sight, and that nobody wants to revive. This enlargement of the literary field, produced by the internal logic of geographical inquiry, took me entirely by surprise: the new method was demanding new data – but those data did not exist yet, and I was not sure how to find them, and the present book takes only a few steps in the new direction. But it's a wonderful challenge, for all cultural historians.

In the meantime, what do literary maps allow us to see? Two things, basically. First, they highlight the *ortgebunden*,[2] place-bound nature of literary forms: each of them with its peculiar geometry, its boundaries, its spatial taboos and favorite routes. And then, maps bring to light the *internal* logic of narrative: the semiotic domain around which a plot coalesces and self-organizes. Literary form appears thus as the result of two conflicting, and equally significant forces: one working from the outside, and one from the inside. It is the usual, and at bottom the only real issue of literary history: society, rhetoric, and their interaction.

And here I will stop, because theoretical promises – *qua* promises, not *qua* theoretical – annoy me enormously. In this book, clearly enough, the method is all.[3] But for precisely this reason, it has to be

[2] The expression is Reiner Hausherr's, 'Kunstgeographie – Aufgaben, Grenzen, Möglichkeiten', *Rheinische Vierteljahrsblätter*, XXXIV, 1970, p. 58.
[3] In the course of time, several people have asked me why on earth did I want to *make* maps, instead of analysing those that already exist. Did I really not understand that a map is a text just like any other – and ought to be treated as a text? and didn't I see that here lay its greatest appeal, for literary critics? I understood, I saw – I also read several studies that took maps as one of their objects: John Gillies on Shakespeare (*Shakespeare and the Geography of Difference*, Cambridge University Press, 1994), J. Hillis Miller on Hardy (*Topographies*, Stanford University Press, 1995), Anne McClintock on *King Solomon's Mines* (*Imperial Leather*, Routledge, London 1995), Lawrence Lipking on Milton (*The Genius of the Shore: Lycidas, Ademastor, and the Poetics of Nationalism*, 'PMLA', 1996). But what can I say, maps don't interest me because they can be 'read' more or less like a novel – but because they change *the way* we read novels. The real challenge, for me, is there.

tested in earnest: across the research as a whole: in its capacity (or not) to change the articulation of the literary field, and the nature of interpretive problems. And the judge, as always, is the reader.

2. 'But we have no artistic atlases'

The idea for this work came to me by sheer chance, from a sentence in Braudel's *Mediterranean*[4] that kept coming to my mind during a long car journey in the summer of 1991: we don't have artistic atlases, we don't have artistic atlases, we don't have *literary* atlases ... So – why not try to make one?

In the following years, I devoted to this idea almost all of my time. I studied geography as I had not done since my school years; conducted experimental seminars at Columbia; convinced twenty literary historians to form an editorial committee, which met for two intense days of discussion, in December 1992, thanks to the hospitality of Maristella Lorch, and the Italian Academy for Advanced Studies in the United States; finally, I wrote a long, detailed research project. But I am not gifted in these things, the National Endowment for the Humanities wasn't convinced, the editorial board dissolved, and the atlas vanished from sight. But I still liked the idea, and continued on my own. I narrowed the field to the only area I know something of, which is the nineteenth-century European novel (with a rapid leap backwards to the Spanish picaresque), and this book is the result. Half methodological manifesto, half pragmatic example; interesting, hopefully; and a real pleasure to write. But my hope is that it may restart the wider enterprise of a Historical Atlas of Literature.

[4] 'The cultural waves that the Baroque unfurled upon Europe were probably more deep, full and uninterrupted than those even of the Renaissance [. . .] But how are we to chart their expansion, their tumultuous foreign adventures, without the indispensable maps that no one has yet constructed? We have museum catalogues, but no artistic atlases . . .' (Fernand Braudel, *The Mediterranean and the Mediterranean World in the Age of Philip II*, 1949, California University Press, 1995, p. 835.)

In the meantime, I also made the humbling discovery that I was far from the first to have had such a good idea. The possibility of 'a literary-historical atlas of Italy', for instance, had already been sketched by Carlo Dionisotti – the author of *Geografia e storia della letteratura italiana* – in an article of 1970.[5] And in fact, a little research uncovered quite a few of such atlases: the first one, J.G. Bartholomew's *Literary and Historical Atlas of Europe*, had been published as early as 1910 (and reprinted often until 1936); in 1964, it had been the turn of a *Guide littéraire de la France*; in 1973, Michael Hardwick's *Literary Atlas and Gazetteer of the British Isles*; in 1979, David Daiches' *Literary Landscapes of the British Isles: A Narrative Atlas*; then the *Atlas zur deutschen Literatur*, in 1983, edited by Horst Dieter Schlosser; the *Grand Atlas des Littératures*, in 1990, edited by Gilles Quinsat and Bernard Cerquiglini; and finally, in 1996, *The Atlas of Literature*, edited by Malcolm Bradbury.[6] All quite different, and all written (a fact I find a little hard to believe) as if in total ignorance of each other's existence; but all with one thing in common: maps play in them a wholly peripheral role. Decorative. There are quite a few of them, by all means, especially in the more recent books: but they are colorful appendixes, that don't intervene in the interpretive process; at times, they even show up at the end of the text – when the discourse is over, done with.

As readers must have already guessed, this in my view is a mistake. Placing a literary phenomenon in its specific space – mapping it – is not the conclusion of geographical work; it's the *beginning*. After which begins in fact the most challenging part of the whole enterprise: one looks at the map, *and thinks*. You look at a specific configuration – those roads that run towards Toledo and Sevilla; those

---

[5] 'Culture regionali e letteratura nazionale in Italia', *Lettere Italiane*, April–June 1970, p. 134.

[6] *A Literary and Historical Atlas of Europe*, Dent, London 1910; *Guide littéraire de la France*, Hachette, Paris 1964; *Literary Atlas and Gazetteer of the British Isles*, Gale Research, Detroit 1973; *Literary Landscapes of the British Isles: A Narrative Atlas*, Paddington Press, New York 1979; *Atlas zur deutschen Literatur*, Deutscher Taschenbuch Verlag, München 1983; *Grand Atlas des Littératures*, Encyclopaedia Universalis, Paris 1990; *The Atlas of Literature*, De Agostini, London 1996. An *Atlas of Western Art History* has also recently been published (John Steer and Anthony White, eds, Facts on File, New York 1994).

mountains, such a long way from London; those men and women that live on opposite banks of the Seine – you look at these patterns, and try to understand how it is that all this gives rise to a story, a plot. How is it, I mean, *that geography shapes the narrative structure of the European novel.*

Think of the maps in this *Atlas* as points of departure, then: for my reflections, as well as yours (a good map should allow for more than one line of thought); and also for the (many) captions which sketch a further array of interpretive paths: towards a text, a critical idea, a historical thesis. Coordinating these intersecting, verbal-visual discourses has not always been easy; the rhythm may be rough, uneven. But I like to think that even so (and even, alas, with all the mistakes that are certainly present) this book may turn out to be *useful*: an adjective that I had never dreamt of applying to myself – and of which I have now grown extremely proud.

If the book really is useful, the credit should go first of all to Serge Bonin. After having directed a work which is a wonder of complexity and rigor – the *Atlas de la Révolution Française* – Bonin has been graceful enough to offer his help to a total amateur like myself; has discussed in detail every single map of the book; has suggested improvements, alternatives, solutions that would never have occurred to me (and that I have followed as often as possible). Bonin has taught me to think with the instruments of cartography; wonderful, like learning another language. And he has convinced me to shun the cheap pleasures of color for the jansenistic clarity of black and white. To say that I am grateful, is a colossal understatement.

I am also grateful to David Kastan and Martin Meisel, who in 1992, at Columbia, came up with some funds without which who knows whether the project would ever have started; and it certainly wouldn't have gone very far without the generous and intelligent help of the research librarians of Columbia, NYU, the Map Division of the New York Public Library, and the Società Geografica Italiana. In the last few years, I have also presented small parts of this work in several American and European universities; my thanks to all those who have discussed with me in those occasions, and during my classes at Columbia; and also to Irene Babboni, John Brenkman, Keith Clarke, Joe Cleary, Margaret Cohen, Robert Darnton, Ernesto Franco, David Lipscomb, Sharon Marcus, Michael Matin, D.A. Miller, Christopher Prendergast, and James Raven. And then, those with whom I have exchanged ideas during the entire span of the project: Perry Anderson, with his passion for large frescoes, and the intense seriousness that is so peculiarly his; Carlo Ginzburg, who has made fun of my project for years, like those movie coaches that have to wake up a lazy boxer; Francis Mulhern, who has explained to me in detail what worked, and what didn't, and why; Beniamino Placido, who has introduced me to books I would have never known; and Teri Reynolds, who opens my eyes every day to the many bizarre possibilities that are the best thing work and life have to offer.

In retrospect, Braudel's influence on the genesis of this book had been prepared by several previous readings. Kristin Ross' book on Rimbaud, for instance, *The Emergence of Social Space*, with its reflections on the relationships between geography and the literary imagination; or the work of Fredric Jameson, who has always 'seen' culture in spatial terms – be that the double plot of *The Betrothed* or Chandler's Los Angeles, the *Geopolitical Aesthetics*, postmodern 'cognitive mapping', Greimas' semiotic square, the rise of the Japanese novel ... Further back in time, I can see Marco D'Eramo showing me Bourdieu's maps of *Sentimental Education* (and I am really struck, but unsure what to do with them). Further back still, a summer night in London, in the mid 1970s, staying up to read from beginning to end Perry Anderson's *Considerations on Western Marxism*: and in the very first pages, that describe the territorial distribution of Marxist thinkers, I suddenly see how geography may explain the history of culture (but then, to really understand it, I must wait twenty years). And finally, much further back, the most important scene of all, which must have taken place on a Sunday morning towards the end of the 1950s, in Rome: four large marble maps of the Mediterranean, walled into the bastion that encloses the

Forum, in Via dei Fori Imperiali; and my father, who explains to me what they mean. This book was begun on that day.

Chapter 1
The novel, the nation-state

1. Jane Austen's Britain

△ beginnings
○ endings

1. *Northanger Abbey*
2. *Sense and Sensibility*
3. *Pride and Prejudice*
4. *Mansfield Park*
5. *Emma*
6. *Persuasion*

Neighbours in Jane Austen are not the people actually living nearby; they are the people living a little less nearby, who, in social recognition, can be visited. What she sees across the land is a network of propertied houses and families, and through the holes of this tightly drawn mesh most actual people are simply not seen. To be face-to-face in this world is already to belong to a class [. . .] The country [. . .] becomes real only as it relates to the houses which are the real nodes.

RAYMOND WILLIAMS, *The Country and the City*

1. *Home-land*

Let me begin with a map of very well-known novels: figure 1, which shows the places where Jane Austen's plots (or more exactly, their central thread, the heroine's story) begin and end. *Northanger Abbey*, for instance, begins at Fullerton and ends at Woodston; *Sense and Sensibility*, at Norland Park and at Delaford; and so on for the others (except *Persuasion*, whose endpoint is left rather vague). Please take a few moments to look at the figure, because in the end this is what literary geography is all about: you select a textual feature (here, beginnings and endings), find the data, put them on paper – and then you look at the map. In the hope that the visual construct will be more than the sum of its parts: that it will show a shape, a pattern that may *add* something to the information that went into making it.

And a pattern does indeed emerge here: of exclusion, first of all. No Ireland; no Scotland; no Wales; no Cornwall. No 'Celtic fringe', as Michael Hechter has called it;[1] only England: a much smaller space than the United Kingdom as a whole. And not even all of England: Lancashire, the North, the industrial revolution – all missing. Instead, we have here the much older England celebrated by the 'estate poems' of topographical poetry: hills, parks, country houses ... (figure 2). It's a first instance of what literary geography may tell us: two things at once: what *could* be in a novel – and what actually *is*

[1] Michael Hechter, *Internal Colonialism. The Celtic Fringe in British National Development, 1836–1966*, University of California Press, Berkeley–Los Angeles 1975.

there. On the one hand, the industrializing 'Great' Britain of Austen's years; on the other, the small, homogeneous England of Austen's novels.

A small England, I have said. Smaller than the United Kingdom, to be sure; and small for us, now. Less so, however, at the turn of the eighteenth century, when the places on the map were separated by a day, or more, of very uncomfortable travel. And since these places coincide with the residences of the heroine (the beginning), and that of her husband-to-be (the ending), the distance between them means that Austen's plots join together – 'marry' – people *who belong to*

---

2. 'Estate poems' 1650–1850

Estate poems – which describe and celebrate a country estate – are most frequent in the southern counties of England where Austen's novels typically take place, while the 'Celtic periphery' is again virtually absent.

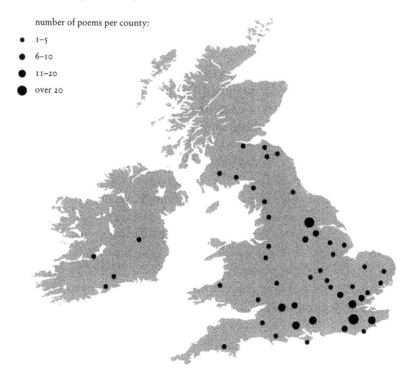

number of poems per county:

●   1–5

●   6–10

●   11–20

●   over 20

different counties. Which is new, and significant: it means that these novels try to represent what social historians refer to as the 'National Marriage Market': a mechanism that crystallized in the course of the eighteenth century, which demands of human beings (and especially of women) a new mobility: physical, and even more so *spiritual* mobility. Because it is clear that a large marriage market can only work if women feel 'at home' – in figure 1, many of the names indicate homes – not only in the small enclave of their birth, but in a much wider territory.[2] If they can feel the nation-state as a true home-land – and if not the nation-state as a whole, at least its 'core area', as social geography calls it: the wealthiest, most populated area (and the safest one, where a young woman may move around without fear). *Northanger Abbey*:

> Charming as were all Mrs. Radcliffe's works, and charming even as were the works of all her imitators, it was not in them perhaps that human nature, at least in the midland counties of England, was to be looked for. Of the Alps and the Pyrenees, with their pine forests and their vices, they might give a faithful delineation; and Italy, Switzerland, and the south of France, might be as fruitful in horrors as they were represented. Catherine dared not doubt beyond her own country, and even of that, if hard pressed, would have yielded the northern and western extremities [the Celtic Fringe!]. But in the central part of England there was surely some security for the existence even of a wife not beloved, in the laws of the land, and the manner of the age . . .
> *Northanger Abbey*, 25[3]

But in the central part of England . . . There is no better title for the map of Austen's novels. And as for Radcliffe's imitators, figure 3 (on the following page) shows the wide gulf separating the world of the Gothic from that of Catherine Morland.

---

[2] Austen's space is of course too obviously *English* to be truly representative of the *British* nation. In this respect, Edgeworth's *The Absentee* (1812), or Ferrier's *Marriage* (1818), that deal with Ireland and Scotland as well as England, provide a more complete geographical setting (although in the end Edgeworth and Ferrier return to the idea of the nation within the nation, relinquishing the corruption of England for Ireland and Scotland respectively). The point is that England has long enjoyed an ambiguous and privileged position within the United Kingdom: *part* of it (like Scotland, Ireland, Wales) – but a *dominant* part, that claims the right to stand in for the whole. Austen's geo-narrative system is an extremely successful version of this opaque overlap of England and Britain.

[3] Narrative passages are identified by the title of the text, followed by the number of the chapter.

Literary sociology has long insisted, as we know, on the relationship between the novel and capitalism. But Austen's space suggests an equally strong affinity (first pointed out by Benedict Anderson,

---

3. British Gothic tales 1770–1840

In this sample of nearly sixty texts, the highest concentration of Gothic tales is to be found in the triangle comprised between the Rhine, the Black Forest, and the Harz (the region of the pact with the Devil): a geographical distribution that was probably influenced by the enormous number of Gothic texts written in German. In general, Gothic stories were initially set in Italy and France; moved north, to Germany, around 1800; and then north again, to Scotland, after 1820. Except for one tale located in Renaissance London, no other story takes place inside Austen's English space.

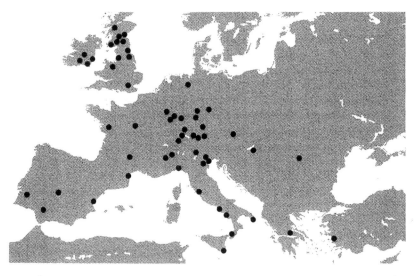

not shown:

● Lebanon

● Ceylon

● setting

Reginald, sole heir of the illustrious family of Di Venoni, was remarkable, from his earliest infancy, for a wild enthusiastic disposition [. . .] The gloomy château in which he resided was situated in Swabia on the borders of the Black Forest. It was a wild isolated mansion, built after the fashion of the day in the gloomiest style of Gothic architecture. At a distance rose the ruins of the once celebrated Castle of Rudstein, of which at present but a mouldering tower remained; and, beyond, the landscape was terminated by the deep shades and impenetrable recesses of the Black Forest . . .

ANONYMOUS, *The Astrologer's Prediction or The Maniac's Fate* (1826)

in *Imagined Communities*) between the novel and the geo-political reality of the nation-state. A modern reality, the nation-state – and a curiously elusive one. Because human beings can directly grasp most of their habitats: they can embrace their village, or valley, with a single glance; the same with the court, or the city (especially early on, when cities are small and have walls); or even the universe – a starry sky, after all, is not a bad image of it. But the nation-state? 'Where' is it? What does it look like? How can one *see* it? And again: village, court, city, valley, universe can all be visually represented – in paintings, for instance: but the nation-state? Well, the nation-state . . . found the novel. And viceversa: the novel found the nation-state. And being the only symbolic form that could represent it, it became an essential component of our modern culture.

Some nation-states (notably England/Britain and France) already existed, of course, long before the rise of the novel: but as 'potential' states, I would say, rather than actual ones. They had a court at the center, a dynasty, a navy, some kind of taxation – but they were hardly integrated systems: they were still fragmented into several local circuits, where the strictly *national* element had not yet affected everyday existence. But towards the end of the eighteenth century a number of processes come into being (the final surge in rural enclosures; the industrial take-off; vastly improved communications; the unification of the national market; mass conscription) that literally drag human beings out of the local dimension, and throw them into a much larger one. Charles Tilly speaks of a new value for this period – 'national loyalty' – that the state tries to force above and against 'local loyalties'.[4] He is right, I believe, and the clash of old and new loyalty shows also how much of a *problem* the nation-state initially was: an unexpected coercion, quite unlike previous power relations; a wider, more abstract, more enigmatic dominion – *that needed a new symbolic form in order to be understood.*
And here, Austen's novelistic geography shows all its intelligence. In a striking instance of the problem-solving vocation of

---

[4] Charles Tilly, *Coercion, Capital, and European States*, Blackwell, Cambridge–Oxford 1990, p. 107.

literature, her plots take the painful reality of territorial uprooting – when her stories open, the family abode is usually on the verge of being lost – and rewrite it as a seductive journey: prompted by desire, and crowned by happiness. They take a *local* gentry, like the Bennets of *Pride and Prejudice*, and join it to the *national* elite of Darcy and his ilk.[5] They take the strange, harsh novelty of the modern state – and turn it into a large, exquisite home.

2. England and its double

Marriage market, then. Like every other market, this also must take place somewhere, and figure 4 shows where: London, Bath, the seaside. Here people meet to complete their transactions, and here is also where all the trouble of Austen's universe occurs: infatuations, scandals, slanders, seductions, elopements – disgrace. And all of this happens because the marriage market (again, like every other market) has produced its own brand of swindlers: shady relatives, social climbers, speculators, seducers, déclassé aristocrats . . .

It makes sense, then, that this figure should be the inverse of figure 1. Look at them: the former is an introverted, rural England: an island within an island. The latter opens up to the sea, the great mix of Bath, and London, the busiest city in the world. In one, a scattered distribution of independent estates: in the other, an ellipse with one focus in London, and the other in Bath. There, homes; here, cities: and cities that are all real, whereas those homes were all fictional: an asymmetry of the real and the imaginary – of geography, and literature – that will recur throughout the present research.[6]

---

[5] On the two gentries, see Lawrence Stone and Jeanne C. Fawtier Stone, *An Open Elite? England 1540–1880*, Oxford University Press, 1986, passim.

[6] Why do novels so often mix real geographical sites and imaginary locations? Are the latter needed for some *specific* narrative function? Are there, in other words, events that tend to happen in real spaces – and others that 'prefer' fictional ones? It is early to give a definitive answer, but Austen's novels certainly suggest that fictional spaces are particularly suited to happy endings, and the wish-fulfillment they usually embody. By contrast, the more pessimistic a narrative structure becomes, the more infrequent are its imaginary spaces.

4. Jane Austen's Britain

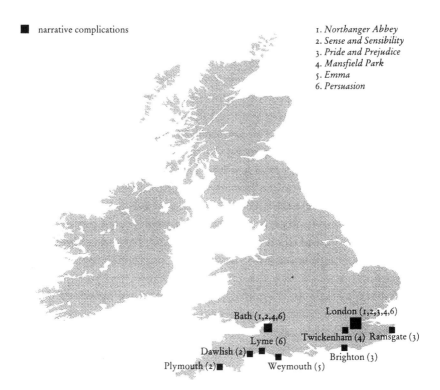

■   narrative complications

1. *Northanger Abbey*
2. *Sense and Sensibility*
3. *Pride and Prejudice*
4. *Mansfield Park*
5. *Emma*
6. *Persuasion*

Bath (1,2,4,6)   London (1,2,3,4,6)

Lyme (6)   Twickenham (4)   Ramsgate (3)

Dawlish (2)   Brighton (3)

Plymouth (2)   Weymouth (5)

About a year ago, [my sister] was taken from school, and an establishment formed for her in London; and last summer she went with the lady who presided over it, to Ramsgate; and thither also went Mr Wickham, undoubtedly by design; for there proved to have been a prior acquaintance between him and Mrs Younge, in whose character were most unhappily deceived; and by her connivance and aid, he so far recommended himself to Georgiana, whose affectionate heart retained a strong impression of his kindness to her as a child, that she was persuaded to believe herself in love, and to consent to an elopement. She was then but fifteen . . .

JANE AUSTEN, *Pride and Prejudice*, 35

Two Englands, where different narrative and axiological functions are literally 'attached' to different spaces (figure 5): and which
one will prevail? The élite that has preserved its rural and local roots
– or the mobile, urbanized group of seducers? In the language of the
age: Land, or Money? We know Austen's answer: Land (preferably,
with plenty of Money). But more significant than the final choice
between the two spaces is the preliminary fact that Austen's England
is not one. The novel functions as the symbolic form of the nation-
state, I said earlier: and it's a form that (unlike an anthem, or a monument) not only does not conceal the nation's internal divisions, *but
manages to turn them into a story*. Think of the two Englands of
figure 5: they form a field of narrative forces, whose reiterated inter-
play defines the nation *as the sum of all its possible stories*: London, or
the painful complications of life; the countryside, or the peace of clos-
ure; the seaside, and illicit emotions; Scotland, for secret lovers; Ireland and the Highlands, who knows, perhaps lands of the Gothic . . .

Austen's England; what an invention. And I say invention delib-
erately, because today the spatial scope of her novels may strike us as
obvious, but historically it wasn't obvious at all. Readers needed a
symbolic form capable of making sense of the nation-state, I have
often repeated; they needed it, yes – but, before Austen, no one had
really come up with it. Look at figure 6: the travels of the heroine and
the other main characters in Amelie Opie's *Adeline Mowbray*. Space,
here, is so stretched as to be almost shapeless: in one novel, the heroine and the other characters travel as much as in Austen's six novels
taken together (figure 7) – a choice which has its own *raison d'être* (a
woman who defies current morality will suffer an endless *via crucis*:
in Lisbon, in Perpignan, in Richmond, in London . . .), but that certainly cannot turn the nation into a symbolic 'home'. Or again, look
at figure 8: the 'excellent tale of *Manouvering*', as Scott calls it in the
preface to *Ivanhoe*. Here, we have the opposite configuration to
Opie's: the two heroines are motionless, in Devon, inside two neigh-
boring estates – while their men sail all over the world. A very simple,
very clear division of the narrative universe: women at home, and
men abroad (while the nation is again lost from sight).

5. Jane Austen's Britain

▲   beginnings

●   endings

■   narrative complications

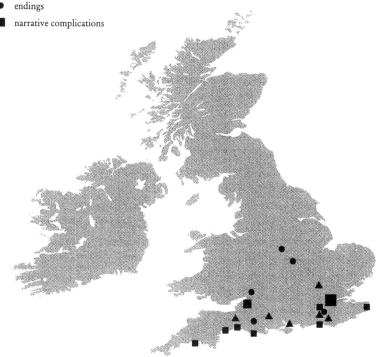

All late-eighteenth-century moralists of whatever colour-
ing prefer the country to the town, but Jane Austen's
Fanny does so as a typical conservative: because she associates it with a community, in which individuals have
well-defined duties towards the group, and because physically it reminds her of the wider ordered universe to
which the lesser community belongs. Urban life, on the
other hand, has given Mary selfish values: she betrays her
egotism when she laughs at the farmers who will not let
her have a wagon to move her harp ...

MARILYN BUTLER, *Jane Austen and the War of Ideas*

Austen's geography is really different: it's a middle-sized world, much larger than Edgeworth's estate, and much smaller than Opie's Atlantic. It is the typically *intermediate* space of the nation-state, 'large enough to survive and to sharpen its claws on its neighbors, but small enough to be organized from one center and to feel itself as an entity', as Kiernan once put it.[7] A contingent, intermediate construct (large enough … small enough …): and perhaps, it is also because she saw this new space that Austen is still read today, unlike so many of her rivals.

In Austen's middle-sized world, the notion of 'distance' acquires in its turn a new meaning. In Opie, or Edgeworth (or Susannah Gunning, Mary Charlton, Barbara Hofland, Selina Davenport: in fact, in most sentimental fiction), distance is an absolute, ontological category: the loved one is Here – or Away. At Home, or in the Wide World. Present, or Absent (and probably Dead). It's still the atmosphere of Greek romances: space as a mythical force, against whose power of separation human beings (and especially women, from whose viewpoint the story is told) have only one weapon: constancy. They must remain what they are, despite all distance; they must remain loyal, patient – *faithful*.

Against this veritable ideology of space, Austen's heroines discover concrete, Relative Distance. Willoughby, Darcy, are twenty miles away, forty, sixty; so is London, or Portsmouth. Maybe there will be a visit, maybe not, because it takes time and effort to travel forty miles. But this moderate uncertainty shows that distance has been brought down to earth: it can be measured, understood; it is no

[7] V.G. Kiernan, 'State and Nation in Western Europe', *Past and Present*, July 1965, p. 35.

6–8. Britain and the world

In early nineteenth-century sentimental novels the international (and especially Atlantic) space takes the form of long retrospective narratives that focus on the (predominantly male) subplots: wars at sea, long-distance trade, Indian nabobs, West Indian planters …

Compared to her contemporaries, Austen markedly increases the central (and 'English') axis of the plot, so that the significance of the international subplot is accordingly reduced.

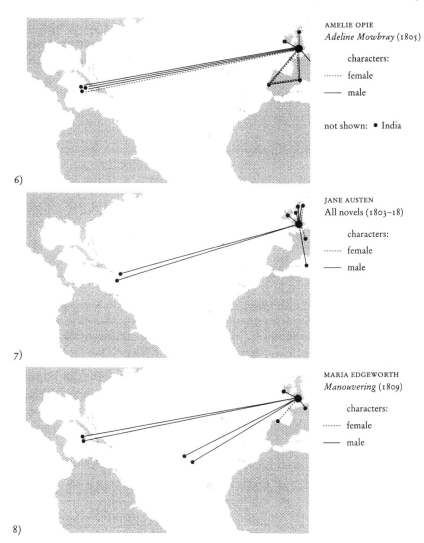

AMELIE OPIE
Adeline Mowbray (1805)

characters:
.... female
——— male

not shown: • India

6)

JANE AUSTEN
All novels (1803–18)

characters:
.... female
——— male

7)

MARIA EDGEWORTH
Manouvering (1809)

characters:
.... female
——— male

8)

H.M.S. l'Ambuscade

Honoured Parents,
I write this from the sea, lat. N.44.15 – long. W.9.45 – wind NNE – to let you know you
will not see me so soon as I said in my last, of the 16th. Yesterday, P.M. two o'clock, some
despatches were brought to my good captain, by the Pickle sloop, which will tomorrow,
wind and weather permitting, alter our destination. What the nature of them is I cannot
impart to you [. . .] For my own part, I long for an opportunity of fighting the French . . .

MARIA EDGEWORTH, *Manouvering*

longer a function of Fate, but of sentiment. It is one more way to attach a meaning to the national space, by literally 'projecting' emotions upon it. When Darcy, who should be in London, shows up at Longbourn, 'a smile of delight added lustre to [Elizabeth's] eyes' (*Pride and Prejudice*, 53). If he has come this far ...

3. *'The recent losses in the West India estate'*

England, Great Britain, the national marriage market, London, Bath, the Celtic fringe . . . And the colonies? Edward Said, 'Jane Austen and Empire':

> In *Mansfield Park*, [. . .] references to Sir Thomas Bertram's overseas possessions are threaded through; they give him his wealth, occasion his absences, fix his social status at home and abroad, and make possible his values [. . .]
>
> What sustains this life materially is the Bertram estate in Antigua [. . .] no matter how isolated and insulated the English place (e.g., Mansfield Park), it requires overseas sustenance [. . .] The Bertrams could not have been possible without the slave trade, sugar, and the colonial planter class.[8]

The Bertrams could not have been possible ... I like the directness of the claim, but disagree with it. I disagree, that is, not with the fact that the British colonies were very profitable, and very ruthlessly run: but with the idea that the English ruling class would 'not have been possible' without them. Take Antigua away, suggests Said, and Sir Bertram disappears: no 'wealth', no 'social status at home and abroad', no 'values', no 'material support', no 'sustenance'. But is this truly the case?

The argument, here, has clearly two sides: the economic role of the British empire – and its fictional representation. On the former, which is far from my field of work, I can only say that I have been convinced by those historians for whom the colonies played certainly a significant, but not an *indispensable* role in British economic

---

[8] Edward Said, *Culture and Imperialism*, Knopf, New York 1993, pp. 62, 85, 89, 94.

life.[9] And this is even truer for the gentry of Northamptonshire (the county of Mansfield Park), which according to Stone and Stone, between 1600 and 1800 engaged in business activities (including colonial investment) in a percentage that oscillated *between one and two percent*:

> The degree to which local landed elites were composed of men enriched in any way by business activities was always negligible. [. . .] Evidence of infiltration, interaction, marriage, entrepreneurship, and other kinds of intermingling were fairly low up to 1879.[10]

---

[9] In general, the key historical question (somewhat removed from *Mansfield Park* itself) is whether colonial profits financed the industrial revolution or not: and whether, as a consequence, the take-off of European capitalism would have been at all possible without colonial possessions. On this point, the arguments I have found most persuasive are those by Patrick K. O'Brien ('The Costs and Benefits of British Imperialism', *Past and Present*, 120, 1988), V.G. Kiernan (*Imperialism and its Contradictions*, Routledge, New York–London 1995), and Paul Bairoch (*Economics and World History*, Chicago University Press, 1993); although Robin Blackburn's *The Making of New World Slavery. From the Baroque to the Modern* (Verso, London 1997), which I read when this book had already been finished, made me reconsider several things.

Kiernan (who is, of course, a vitriolic critic of British imperialism) argues for instance that 'the spoils of Bengal [. . .] *may* have percolated by devious channels into Lancashire mills, but not quite as promptly [as to start the industrial revolution]': and he then proceeds to point out that if early industrialists 'had little access to the big money, they had, however [given the modest financial needs of the industrial take-off] equally little need of it' (pp. 54–5). As for Paul Bairoch, the thesis that the exploitation of the Third World financed the industrial revolution is for him one of the 'myths' of economic history, and his own conclusions turn the argument on its head: 'during the 18th and 19th centuries colonization was primarily a result of industrial development and not vice versa' (p. 82). As Bairoch himself explains at length, however, the myth is so widely accepted because 'if the West did not gain much from colonialism, it does not mean that the Third World did not lose much' (p. 85). In other words, although the Third World did not contribute much to the industrial revolution, the latter, by contrast, had catastrophic effects on the Third World itself (as in the case of de-industrialization, to which Bairoch devotes an entire chapter of his book).

For his part, Blackburn shows in great detail the exceptional profits arising out of West Indian slave plantations, and summarizes his findings in the following way: 'We have seen that the pace of capitalist industrialization in Britain was decisively advanced by its success in creating a regime of extended primitive accumulation and battening upon the super-exploitation of slaves in the Americas. Such a conclusion certainly does not imply that Britain followed some optimum path of accumulation in this period [. . .] nor does our survey lead to the conclusion that New World slavery produced capitalism. What it does show is that exchanges with the slave plantations helped British capitalism to make a breakthrough to industrialism and global economy ahead of its rivals' (p. 572).

[10] Stone and Fawtier Stone, *An Open Elite?* pp. 141, 189. See also the chart on p. 141.

Thus economic history. And if we then turn to *Mansfield Park* itself, Said's thesis becomes even more dubious. Early in the novel, when Bertram's older son runs into debt, his gambling 'robs Edmund for ten, twenty, thirty years, perhaps for life, of more than half the income which ought to be his' (*Mansfield Park*, 3). On the other hand, the 'recent losses in the West India estate', that are mentioned in the very same page, leave no trace on the life at Mansfield Park: losses or not, everything remains exactly the same. Perhaps that estate was not so indispensable after all? And then, here is Bertram, back from Antigua:

> It was a busy morning with him. Conversation with any of them occupied but a small part of it. He had to reinstate himself in all the wanted concerns of his Mansfield life, to see his steward and his bailiff – to examine and compute – and, in the intervals of business, to walk into his stables and his gardens, and nearest plantations.
>
> *Mansfield Park*, 20

To examine and compute, to walk into stables and plantations, to meet the steward and the bailiff (who are in charge of managing the estate, of collecting rents, and of financial affairs in general) . . . All signs of large economic interests *in Britain*, and most likely near Mansfield Park itself. Said's picture seems exactly reversed: modest colonial profits – and large national ones. And yet, when all is said, Bertram *does* indeed leave for Antigua, and stays away for a very long time. If Antigua is not essential to his finances – why on earth does he go?

He goes, not because he needs the money, but because Austen needs him out of the way. Too strong a figure of authority, he intimidates the rest of the cast, stifling narrative energy, and leaving Austen without a story to tell: for the sake of the plot, he must go. It is the difference, as Russian Formalists would say, between the 'function' and the 'motivation' of a narrative episode: between the *consequences* of Bertram's absence (the play, the flirt between Edmund and Mary, Maria's adultery: in short, *virtually the entire plot of the novel*), and its premises: which are far less important, because (as in Freudian 'rationalization', which is a very similar concept) one 'reason' can always be replaced by another without much difficulty.

Bertram goes to Antigua, then, not because he must go *there* – but because *he must leave Mansfield Park*. But it's nevertheless to Antigua that he goes, and I must still account for Austen's specific motivation of her plot. And then, in sentimental novels at the turn of the century, the colonies are a truly ubiquitous presence: they are mentioned in two novels out of three, and overseas fortunes add up to one third, if not more, of the wealth in these texts (figure 9). Why this insistence? Could it be a 'realistic' feature of nineteenth-century narrative, as Said suggests for Jane Austen?

Possibly. But, frankly, these fictional fortunes are so out of proportion to economic history that I suspect them to be there not so much because of reality, but for strictly *symbolic* reasons. Because Jamaica, or Bengal, remove the production of wealth to faraway worlds, in whose effective reality most nineteenth-century readers were probably not 'at all interested' (like Fanny's cousins: see *Mansfield Park*, 21).[11] The way in which colonial fortunes are introduced – a few hasty commonplaces, period – is itself a good clue to the real state of affairs; and as for the colonies themselves, *not one of the thirteen novels of figure 9 represents them directly*; at most, we get a retrospective (and dubious) tale like Rochester's in *Jane Eyre*. This is the mythic geography – *pecunia ex machina* – of a wealth that is not really produced (nothing is ever said of work in the colonies), but magically 'found' overseas whenever a novel needs it. And so, among other things, the link between the wealth of the élite and the 'multitude of labouring poor' of contemporary England can be easily severed: the élite is cleared, innocent. Which is a wonderful thing to know, for heroines that want to marry into it – and even better, of course, in the decades of the harshest class struggle of modern British history.

---

[11] Around 1800, *The Lady's Magazine* devotes hundreds of pages to tales and 'anecdotes' of the colonial world – but provides only a couple of genuine news items (see below, figures 22–25).

9. Colonial wealth in British sentimental novels

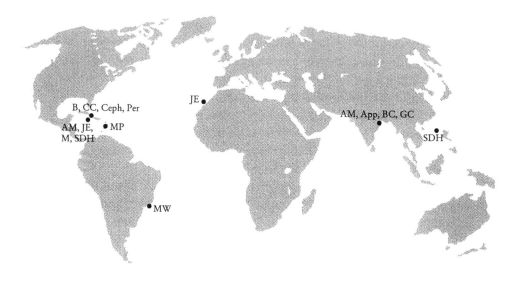

Novels included:

AM	Amelie Opie *Adeline Mowbray*	JE	Charlotte Brontë *Jane Eyre*
App	Amelie Opie *Appearance Was Against Her*	M	Maria Edgeworth *Manouvering*
B	Maria Edgeworth *Belinda*	MP	Jane Austen *Mansfield Park*
BC	Mrs Ross *The Balance of Comfort*	MW	Barbara Hofland *The Merchant's Widow*
CC	anonymous *The Castle on the Cliff*	Per	Jane Austen *Persuasion*
Ceph	anonymous *Cephisa*	SDH	Emily Eden *The Semi-Detached House*
GC	Susannah Gunning *The Gypsy Countess*		

I have received a letter [. . .] from my father-in-law, in
Jamaica, authorizing me to draw on his banker for 900L.,
and inviting me to come over to him; as he feels himself
declining, and wishes to give me the care of his estate, and
of my son, to whom all fortune will descend; and of whose
interest, he properly thinks, no one can be so likely to take
good care as his own father.

AMELIE OPIE, *Adeline Mowbray*

Disavowal: this is the true meaning of figure 9. It is not economic history that explains it, but ideology: an ideology that *projects*, literally, an uncomfortable reality away from Britain. And indeed . . .

4. *Geography of ideas*

. . . indeed, something else is often located abroad, in British novels: villains (figure 10). But the horizon has narrowed: from the Caribbean and Bengal, to France: an enemy just a few miles away, in full view – and so much more effective. This is the strictly national*is*-*tic* aspect of British fiction. Perry Anderson:

> The sense of national community, systematically orchestrated by the State, may well have been a greater reality in the Napoleonic epoch than at any time in the previous century [. . .] The prime weapon in the ideological arsenal [of the British ancien régime], after twenty years of victorious fighting against the French revolution and its successor regimes, was a counter-revolutionary nationalism.[12]

And thus Linda Colley, in *Britons*:

> We can plausibly regard Great Britain as an invented nation superimposed, if only for a while, onto much older alignments and loyalties.
>
> It was an invention forged above all by war. Time and time again, war with France brought Britons, whether they hailed from Wales or Scotland or England, into confrontation with an obviously hostile Other, and encouraged them to define themselves collectively against it.[13]

A hostile Other as the source of collective identity. Words that bring to mind another narrative form in which a threatening foreign presence plays a very large role: the Russian novel of ideas. Or better, as figure 11 suggests, the Russian novel of *European*, and indeed *western*-European ideas. Natural science, political theory, philosophy of history, economic utilitarianism: as in Raskolnikov's article in *Crime and Punishment*, which combines Napoleon, Hegel, and Carlyle, modern culture emerges here from only three countries:

[12] Perry Anderson, *Arguments Within British Marxism*, Verso, London 1980, pp. 37–8.
[13] Linda Colley, *Britons. Forging the Nation 1707–1837*, Yale University Press, 1992, p. 5.

10. Villains

The map indicates the origin or destination of some nineteenth-century villains, and the location of major narrative disasters. Although France is clearly the epicenter of the world's evils, the map actually under-represents its symbolic role, in part because France is not always explicitly mentioned (as in the 'foreign country' of Maria Bertram's exile) and in part because anti-French sentiments are conveyed through other means, such as language (villains love to speak French; and Carker, in *Dombey and Son*, 'speaks it like an angel'), or character description.

Significantly, all the 'wrong' erotic choices of the British *Bildungsroman* involve a woman who is either French (Céline Varens in *Jane Eyre*, Laure in *Middlemarch*), or has received a French education (Flora McIvor in *Waverley*, Blanche Amory in *Pendennis*, Dora Spenlow in *David Copperfield*, Estella in *Great Expectations*). Withstanding Parisian seduction becomes thus one of the decisive passage rites of a young Englishman.

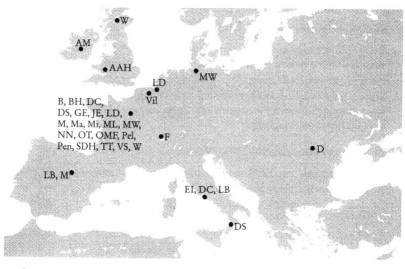

not shown: ● Goa: AAH   ● West Indies: B   ● Jamaica: AM, JE

Novels included:

AAH	Amelie Opie *Appearance Was Against Her*	Ma	Susan Ferrier *Marriage*
AM	Amelie Opie *Adeline Mowbray*	Mi	George Eliot *Middlemarch*
B	Maria Edgeworth *Belinda*	ML	G.P. Reynolds *The Mysteries of London*
BH	Charles Dickens *Bleak House*	MW	Barbara Hofland *The Merchant's Widow*
D	Bram Stoker *Dracula*	NN	Charles Dickens *Nicholas Nickleby*
DC	Charles Dickens *David Copperfield*	OMF	Charles Dickens *Our Mutual Friend*
DS	Charles Dickens *Dombey and Son*	OT	Charles Dickens *Oliver Twist*
EI	Lord Normanby *The English in Italy*	Pel	Edward Bulwer-Lytton *Pelham*
F	Mary Shelley *Frankenstein*	Pen	William Thackeray *Pendennis*
GE	Charles Dickens *Great Expectations*	SDH	Emily Eden *The Semi-Detached House*
JE	Charlotte Brontë *Jane Eyre*	TT	Charles Dickens *A Tale of Two Cities*
LB	Georgiana Fullerton *Lady-Bird*	Vil	Charlotte Brontë *Villette*
LD	Charles Dickens *Little Dorrit*	VS	Lady Blessington *The Victims of Society*
M	Maria Edgeworth *Manouvering*	W	Walter Scott *Waverley*

11. Russian novels of ideas

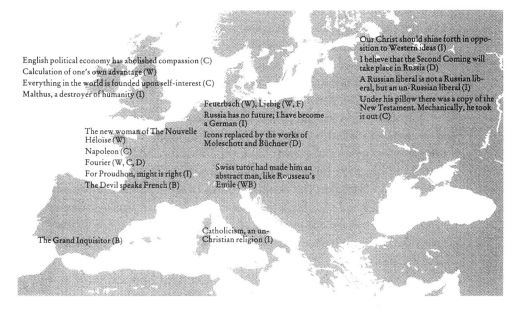

English political economy has abolished compassion (C)
Calculation of one's own advantage (W)
Everything in the world is founded upon self-interest (C)
Malthus, a destroyer of humanity (I)

Our Christ should shine forth in opposition to Western ideas (I)
I believe that the Second Coming will take place in Russia (D)
A Russian liberal is not a Russian liberal, but an un-Russian liberal (I)
Under his pillow there was a copy of the New Testament. Mechanically, he took it out (C)

Feuerbach (W), Liebig (W, F)
Russia has no future; I have become a German (I)
Icons replaced by the works of Moleschott and Büchner (D)

The new woman of The Nouvelle Héloïse (W)
Napoleon (C)
Fourier (W, C, D)
For Proudhon, might is right (I)
The Devil speaks French (B)

Swiss tutor had made him an abstract man, like Rousseau's Emile (WB)

The Grand Inquisitor (B)

Catholicism, an un-Christian religion (I)

Novels included:

B Fyodor Dostoevsky *Brothers Karamazov*
C Fyodor Dostoevsky *Crime and Punishment*
D Fyodor Dostoevsky *The Devils*
F Ivan Turgenev *Fathers and Sons*

I   Fyodor Dostoevsky *The Idiot*
W Nikolai Chernichevsky *What is to be Done?*
WB Alexander Herzen *Who is to be Blame?*

The eighteenth century began with the assertion that the new 'Enlightener' of the Russian land must make a pilgrimage to the West: Peter's 'Great Embassy'. Later, a trip to Paris for the eighteenth-century Russian nobleman acquired the character of a pilgrimage to holy places. Correspondingly, the opponents of Westernization saw such journeys as the primary source of evil. Communion with the Enlightenment [. . .] was accomplished by a simple movement in space.

JURII M. LOTMAN AND BORIS A. USPENSKII, *Binary Models in the Dynamics of Russian Culture (to the End of the Eighteenth Century)*

France, Germany, Britain.[14] And as ideas move eastwards from this 'advanced' Europe, they acquire symbolic momentum, becoming extreme, intransigent: 'what is only a hypothesis in Europe', says Ivan in *Brothers Karamazov*, 'becomes at once an axiom with a Russian boy' (V.3); and Porfiry, in *Crime and Punishment*: 'This is a case that involves dreams derived from books, sir; a heart that has been overstimulated by theories' (VI.2).

A murder derived from dreams and books . . . In Russia, European ideas are not just ideas: they are 'overstimulated' forces, that lead people to action – and crime. Like the French villains of figure 10, European ideas are therefore treated as a genuine threat to all that is most deeply Russian: the religious faith (and folly) of the eastern margin of figure 11, completed east of the Urals in Raskolnikov's religious rebirth on the banks of the Irtysh. And yet, these writers never really rescind their connection with Europe; not even Dostoevsky, despite all his ambivalence. For them, Western ideas embody the cynicism of modernity, but also its greatness: ideas as lucid and fearless as their spokesmen – Bazarov, Raskolnikov, Ivan Karamazov. Great characters, all of them, and great because *divided*: because the clash between Russia and the West has entered their minds, and resounds in every excited speech, in every unpredictable act (and in all the *'whys?'* that retrospectively chase it, in search of its meaning). It's Bakhtin's 'dialogism': every issue opens up to opposite viewpoints, even in the same person. And it's also an instance of how geography may, if not exactly determine, at least *encourage morphological change*: because only a country that was both inside and outside Europe – i.e., only Russia – could call into question modern Western culture, and subject it (with Dostoevsky) to genuine 'experiments'. And indeed only Russia realized the great formal shift of the novel of ideas.

---

[14] More precisely, figure 11 reveals a sort of European division of labour, that recalls the well-known account of the sources of Marxism: from Britain comes political economy, with its ruthless (a)moral consequences; from France, political utopia, and the violence that often accompanies it; from Germany, scientific-philosophical atheism. The great exception to this geography of ideas is Ivan Karamazov's parable of the Great Inquisitor, which is set in Sevilla (but was almost certainly inspired by Schiller's *Don Carlos*).

5. Far from the center

Sentimental novels. Novels of ideas. And now, the most successful form of the century: the historical novel, for which figure 12 – that
mixes a few classic texts, and others which have long been forgotten
– maps out the main areas of action.[15]

Now, we have long ago agreed to call historical novels 'historical'
to emphasize their peculiar relationship to time. But this map suggests that their spatial component is just as striking as their temporal
one. In a negative way, first of all: because this form seems to flourish only *away from the center*. Think of Austen's world: everything
within a circle centering on London (a day, a day-and-a-half away).
Well, historical novels show the opposite pattern: a weak centripetal
pull, with the story running immediately away from the national
capital. The young hero of *The Captain's Daughter*, for instance,
who dreams of going to Petersburg, is promptly dispatched in the
opposite direction, to the eastern periphery of the Czarist empire. In
Waverley, Charles Stewart never completes his march towards
London: he lands in the North-West of Scotland, raises the Standard
of Rebellion in the middle of the Highlands, crosses the Highland
line, reaches Edinburgh, crosses the Anglo-Scottish border, reaches
Derby – and then stops. He stops, in other words, exactly *where
Austen's England begins* (Pemberley, the northernmost locality
'seen' in her novels, is also in Derbyshire). And that Scott's world
should end exactly where Austen's begins, and Austen's end where
Scott's begins . . . such a perfect fit, of course, is only a (beautiful)
coincidence. But behind the coincidence lies a solid reality: namely,

[15] The main areas of action . . . A premise that differs from the one used for Austen
(with its emphasis on beginning, middle, and ending), or for novels of ideas (with their
focus on the paradigmatic opposition of European and Russian ideas). But different forms
have different narrative dominants, and the junctures that are crucial in sentimental novels
– *and therefore also in their cartographic representation* – are not so in historical, or
picaresque, or colonial novels. And then, no map can include everything: to make sense, it
must limit itself to a finite number of factors. In the course of the book I have therefore
attempted a (geographical) elaboration of those (narrative) elements that seemed most relevant to each given form; in this respect, my geography is inseparable from a morphology.

that different forms inhabit different spaces. Paul Zumthor, *La Mesure du monde*:

> Each of the various narrative genres active between the eleventh and the fourteenth centuries possesses its own poetic space, and seems to direct its gaze towards a specific horizon. The amiable French *fabliau* limits itself to a 'here' (the home, the city) whose shadows it investigates with amusement (and at times with some rage); romances, in France and Germany, move by

---

12. Historical novels

Unlike sentimental novels, historical novels are usually located in the proximity of major natural barriers: forests (*The Chouans*), hardly accessible coastlines (*Loukis Laras, The Boyne Water*), wide expanses of territory (*The Captain's Daughter, Taras Bulba*), and especially mountains (*Waverley, El señor de Bembibre, The Rose of Disentis, The Golden Age of Transylvania*). Places 'whose history consists in not having one, and remain at the margins of the great currents of civilization' (Braudel), mountains allow historical novels to move quickly and dramatically into the most distant past.

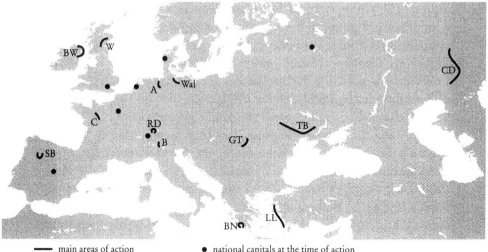

—— main areas of action   • national capitals at the time of action

Novels included:

A Jakob van Lennep *An Abduction in the Seventeenth Century*
BN Henry Moke *The Battle of Navarino*
B Alessandro Manzoni *The Betrothed*
BW John and Michael Banim *The Boyne Water*
CD Alexander Pushkin *The Captain's Daughter*
C Honoré de Balzac *The Chouans*
GT Mór Jókai *The Golden Age of Transylvania*

LL Demetrius Bikelos *Loukis Laras*
RD Heinrich Zschoschke *The Rose of Disentis*
SB Enrique Gil y Carrasco *El señor de Bembibre*
TB Nikolai Gogol *Taras Bulba*
Wal B.S. Ingemann *Waldemar*
W Walter Scott *Waverley*

contrast towards the 'down there' of an uncertain adventure. The epics that specialized singers are still spreading throughout the West focus on the military opposition between Christianity and 'Pagan' lands.[16]

And thus, in more general terms, Mikhail Bakhtin:

> The chronotope in literature has an intrinsic generic significance. It can even be said that it is precisely the chronotope that defines genre and generic distinctions.[17]

Each genre possesses its own space, then – *and each space its own genre*: defined by a spatial distribution – by a map – which is unique to it, and which for historical novels suggests: away from the center. And, by reflex, *in the proximity of borders*: the border between the Dutch Republic and German cities (*An Abduction in the Seventeenth Century*); the Danish kingdom, and the Holy Roman Empire (*Waldemar*); Russians, and Cossacks (*The Captain's Daughter*); Hungarians, and the Ottoman Empire (*The Golden Age of Transylvania*); Greeks, and Turks (*The Battle of Navarino, Loukis Laras*); Protestants, and Catholics (*The Boyne Water*). Far from being accidental, this geographical constant is probably a major factor of the exceptional success of historical novels, because it offers nineteenth-century Europe a veritable *phenomenology of the border*. Which is a great thing to do when borders are simultaneously hardening, and being challenged as 'unnatural' by the various nationalist waves (figure 13) – and when, as a consequence, the need to represent the territorial divisions of Europe grows suddenly stronger.

Borders, then. Of which there are two kinds: external ones, between state and state; and internal ones, within a given state. In the first case, the border is the site of *adventure*: one crosses the line, and is face to face with the unknown, often the enemy; the story enters a space of danger, surprises, suspense. It is so with all the lesser-known novels in figure 12: in *An Abduction in the Seventeenth Century*, for instance, we have the whole machinery of the chase, and in *Loukis*

---

[16] Paul Zumthor, *La Mesure du monde*, Seuil, Paris 1993, p. 382.
[17] Mikhail Bakhtin, 'Forms of Time and of the Chronotope in the Novel', 1937–38, in *The Dialogic Imagination*, Texas University Press, Austin 1981, pp. 84–5.

13. The formation of European borders

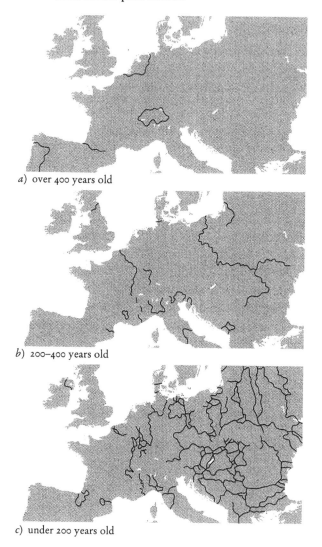

a) over 400 years old

b) 200–400 years old

c) under 200 years old

The idea of the nation, with the ensuing ideology of nationalism, is the result of the establishment of the state within rigorously defined borders, which are as a consequence claimed as such [. . .] An absolute – and, as a rule, unconditioned – sovereignty is wielded by the state upon this delimited territory.

JULIEN FREUND, *L'Ennemi et le tiers dans l'état*

Laras of the flight. In *Waldemar*, the city of Schwerin, in Mecklen-
burg, is won and lost a half-dozen times, just like the Swiss village of
The Rose of Disentis. In *The Golden Age of Transylvania*, mysterious knights; in *The Battle of Navarino*, mysterious captives. And so
on, and so on.

External frontiers, in other words, easily generate narrative – but
in an elementary way: they take two opposite fields, and make them
collide. *Internal* borders work differently, and focus on a theme
which is far less flamboyant than adventure, but much more disturb-
ing: *treason*. Waverley, Taras Bulba's younger son, Balzac's and
Pushkin's heroes, Alvaro de Bembibre, Renzo ('Stay there, you
accursed country!'): all traitors. They all have their reasons, of
course, and their treason may well be unintentional, or due to
entirely unpolitical reasons (curiosity, in Scott and Manzoni; love, in
Balzac and Gogol). Still, in one guise or another, treason is there in all
great historical novels: as the hero reaches the internal border, he
immediately joins the Rebel, the Riot, the Pretender, the *gars*, the
heretics. Rebelliousness? I doubt it, these are 'insipid' young men (as
Scott says of his Waverley), and their actions show rather *how weak
national identity still is*, in nineteenth-century Europe. A struggle
between national and local loyalties, writes Tilly of these years: true,
and treason shows the bitterness of the conflict, which keeps the
hero's soul long suspended – Waverley, wavering – between nation
and region.[18]

Scott's internal border (or Balzac's, or Pushkin's) has yet another
peculiarity: it is not so much a politico-military demarcation, as an
anthropological one. When Waverley leaves his regiment to visit
Tully-Veolan, and then Glennaquoich, in the Highlands, his movement in space is also, and in fact above all, the movement in *time*

---

[18] This dual allegiance is personified in the compromise formation of the Noble Trai-
tor – Fergus, Alvaro de Bembibre, the Marquis de Montauran – with its precarious balance
of adjective and noun. On the one hand, these characters are all enemies of the new centralized power of the state, and the novel, obediently, sentences them to death; but on the
other hand it presents them as generous, young, brave, passionate – 'noble' – thus allowing itself a parting homage to the old ruling class.

visualized in figure 14. He travels backwards through the various stages of social development described by the Scottish Enlightenment: the age of Trade, of Agriculture, of Herding (the pretext for seeing the Highlands is a cattle raid), and finally of Hunting (the essence of Highland culture is embodied in Fergus' ritualized hunting party – which also coincides with the beginning of the rebellion).[19]

Scott's 'ability to read time in space', as Bakhtin put it in his essay on the *Bildungsroman*,[20] is of course a well-known fact – obvious, perhaps. Not obvious, however, is the fact that space does not become time just anywhere, in historical novels, but *only in the proximity of the internal border*. Only there it becomes possible to 'see' a journey into the past – *and thus to imagine the very form of the historical novel, which is itself a journey into the past*. After all, the 'historical' theme was already present in the first draft of *Waverley*, in 1805 (and also in many earlier novels): but without the space of the border something was missing, and 'I threw aside the work I had commenced', writes Scott in the General Preface, 'without either reluctance or remonstrance'. Ten years later he turns to geography, sends his young man to the Highlands – and invents the key genre of the century.

Geography as the foundation of narrative form; the internal border as the on/off switch of the historical novel. And it makes sense, because the internal border is the space where the non-contemporaneity of European countries (and especially of those where trade and industry have advanced more quickly, like France and Great Britain) becomes inescapably visible: a distance of just

---

[19] The opening chapter of *The Golden Age of Transylvania* is entitled 'A Hunt in the year 1666'; elsewhere, anthropological regression is metonymically conveyed by garments of animal skin: *The Chouans'* Marche-à-terre wears goatskins and tree barks; when Pugacev first appears, in *The Captain's Daughter*, he has just lost his sheepskin; and when the hero of *The Rose of Disentis*, Florian Prevost, decides to reclaim his Swiss identity, the first thing he does is to dress as a chamois-hunter. Cooper's hero, needless to say, is also a hunter, nicknamed Leatherstocking.

[20] Mikhail Bakhtin, 'The *Bildungsroman* and its Significance in the History of Realism', in *Speech Genres and other Late Essays*, Texas University Press, 1986, p. 53.

14. Walter Scott, *Waverley*

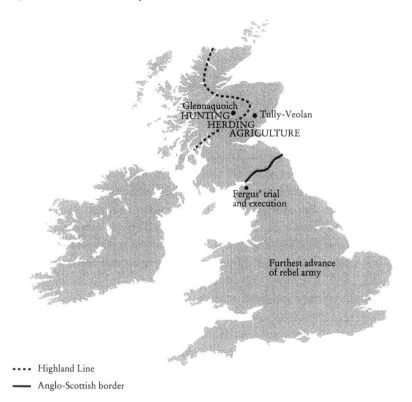

Glennaquoich
HUNTING Tully-Veolan
HERDING
AGRICULTURE

Fergus' trial
and execution

Furthest advance
of rebel army

•••• Highland Line
——— Anglo-Scottish border

There is no European nation, which, within the course of half a century, or little more, has undergone so complete a change as this kingdom of Scotland. The effects of the insurrection of 1745, – the destruction of the patriarchal power of the Highland chiefs, – the abolition of the heritable jurisdiction of the Lowland nobility and barons, – the total eradication of the Jacobite party, which, averse to intermingle with the English, or adopt their customs, long continued to pride themselves upon maintaining ancient Scottish manners and costumes, – commenced this innovation. The gradual influx of wealth, and extension of commerce, have since united to render the present people of Scotland a class of beings as different from their grandfathers, as the existing English are from those of Queen Elizabeth's time.

WALTER SCOTT, 'A Postscript', *Waverley*

a few miles, and people belong to different epochs. Internal borders define modern states as composite structures, then, made of many temporal layers: as *historical* states – that need historical novels.

But need them to do what? To represent internal unevenness, no doubt; and then, to *abolish* it. Historical novels are not just stories 'of' the border, but of its erasure, and of the incorporation of the internal periphery into the larger unit of the state: a process that mixes consent and coercion – Love, and War; Nation, and State – as David Lipscomb points out in his discussion of Scott's 'three estates' (figure 15). Love, between the man from England and the woman from the Lowlands estate: a miniature of a national union based on the agreement, the mutual desire of the more 'civilized' spaces. But war (and no prisoners), against the still 'savage' space, so that the state may finally achieve Weber's 'monopoly of legitimate violence', crushing once and for all Pugacev and Fergus and Bonnie Prince Charlie, don Rodrigo and the Signora and the Unnamed, the Chouans and the Cossacks and the Knights of the Temple. State building requires *streamlining*, historical novels tell us: the blotting out of regional borders (Scott, Balzac, Pushkin), and the submission of the Gothic strongholds of old feudal privilege. In *The Betrothed*, Manzoni's divided plot charts both processes at once, moving now towards the future and now towards the past: and while Renzo proceeds to encounter the urban revolt, and the proto-industrial production on the other side of the Adda, Lucia, in her much shorter journey, is the last victim of the convents and towers of old local power (figure 16).

6. *Theoretical interlude I. Of space and style*

Before leaving the historical novel, a methodological point. In the course of my research, I have thought of literary maps as good tools to analyze plot, but not much else, and certainly not style. When working on historical novels, however, I began to wonder. My starting point was an essay by Enrica Villari on the recurrent presence of

15. The incorporation of the Scottish Lowlands in *Waverley* and *Rob Roy*

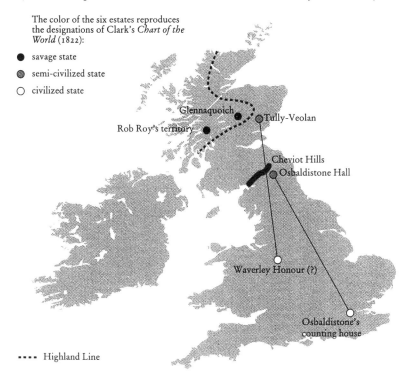

The color of the six estates reproduces
the designations of Clark's *Chart of the
World* (1822):

● savage state

◉ semi-civilized state

○ civilized state

Glennaquoich

Rob Roy's territory

Tully-Veolan

Cheviot Hills

Osbaldistone Hall

Waverley Honour (?)

Osbaldistone's
counting house

•••• Highland Line

In the Waverley novels [. . .] there is a three-estate time-line,
running from a civilized estate [. . .] up the king's highway to a
semi-civilized estate (or the 'Lowland estate') at the base of a
'formidable topographical barrier', and finally over the barrier
to a fully-feudal estate (or the 'Highland estate', the realm of
Fergus, Burley, or Rob Roy) [. . .] The final marriage between
the Waverley hero (who has Hanoverian political ties) and the
Jacobite heiress does not cross the novel's topographical barrier. [. . .] What exactly happens to the Highland space is not
entirely clear, but no doubt it has lost the fearsome aspect that
it first shows to the Waverley hero [. . .] Scottish culture, in the
form of the Lowland estate, is incorporated into the nation, but
Scottish political nationalism is left in the past, on the other side
of the topographical barrier.

DAVID LIPSCOMB, 'Geographies of Progress'

16. The space of *The Betrothed*

'Is it Bergamo, that place?'
'The town of Bergamo', the fisherman replied.
'And that shore, is it Bergamasque?'
'Land of St Mark.'
'Hooray for Saint Mark!!'

ALESSANDRO MANZONI, *The Betrothed*, 17

—— Lucia's story
······ Renzo's story

In *The Betrothed*, the separation of the lovers allows Manzoni to write two very distinct narrative lines which can be read as two different generic modes. The plight of Lucia, for instance, gives him the material for a Gothic novel, in which the feminine victim eludes one trap only to fall into a more agonizing one, confronting villains of ever blacker nature, and providing the narrative apparatus for the development of a semic system of evil and redemption, and for a religious and psychological vision of the fate of the soul. Meanwhile, Renzo wanders through the *grosse Welt* of history and of the displacement of vast armed populations, the realm of the destiny of peoples and vicissitudes of their governments.

FREDRIC JAMESON, *Magical Narratives*

comic and 'tragico-sublime' characters in Scott's world.[21] It's an idea that applies just as well to Pushkin, or Manzoni, and that includes in its turn a marked spatial component: because, again, these characters are not randomly distributed a bit everywhere in the novel, but are usually found in the proximity of the border.[22] But if comic and tragic elements tend to show up near the border, this means that in Scott, or Pushkin, *stylistic choices are determined by a specific geographical position.* Space acts upon style, producing a double deviation (towards tragedy and comedy: towards the 'high' and the 'low') from that average, 'serious', 'realistic' register that is typical of the nineteenth century. Although the novel usually has a very low 'figurality' (as Francesco Orlando would say), near the border *figurality rises:*[23] space and tropes are entwined; rhetoric is dependent upon space. Here, even proper names lose their modern, indexical quality (their 'meaninglessness') and re-acquire a striking semantic intensity: the Son of John the Great, the Deerslayer, the Unnamed, Dead Blood, the Garden of the Devil . . . Not for nothing, in *The Chouans*, the rationalism of revolutionary Paris tries to banish forever the use of Breton nicknames.

A space–trope continuum. Here is what happens to Scott's descriptions – as a rule, implacably analytical – when Waverley approaches the Highlands:

[21] Enrica Villari, 'La resistenza alla storia nei romanzi giacobiti di Walter Scott', in *Storie su storie. Indagine sui romanzi storici (1818–1840)*, Neri Pozza, Verona 1985, especially pp. 16–30.

[22] They also tend to show up always in the same sequence: before the border comic characters, and beyond it tragic ones. A few miles before the Highlands, Cosmo Bradwardine; beyond the Highland Line, Fergus. Before, Pugacev in the garb of a ridiculous old peasant; beyond, Pugacev as the terrifying rebel. On the square of Notre Dame Quasimodo, the Pope of Fools; inside the cathedral Claude Frollo, the ruthless feudal master. On the road, Don Abbondio; inside their feudal enclaves, the Signora and the Innominato. As is to be expected, comic characters belong usually to those spaces that bow to the new central power without too much struggle; tragico-sublime ones, to the spaces of strongest resistance, which are mercilessly crushed.

[23] Francesco Orlando, *For a Freudian Theory of Literature*, 1973, Johns Hopkins University Press, Baltimore and London 1978, especially pp. 164 ff.

The light [. . .] appeared plainly to be a large fire, but whether kindled upon an island or the main land, Edward could not determine. As he saw it, the red glaring orb seemed to rest on the very surface of the lake itself, and resembled the fiery vehicle in which the Evil Genius of an Oriental tale traverses land and sea [. . .] The boat now neared the shore, and Edward could discover that this large fire, amply supplied with branches of pine-wood by two figures who, in the red reflections of its light, appeared like demons, was kindled in the jaws of a lofty cavern . . .

Waverley, 17

The light appeared *plainly* to be a large fire . . . But then, plain style is quickly discarded: glaring orb, fiery vehicle, Evil Genius, demons, jaws . . . The impact with the border has generated a sudden figural leap (much like the 'monsters' of old mapmakers).[24] Then, as soon as the border has been passed:

The interior of the cave, which here rose very high, was illuminated by torches made of pine-tree, which emitted a bright and bickering light, attended by a strong though not unpleasant odour. Their light was assisted by the red glare of a large charcoal fire, round which were seated five or six armed Highlanders, while others were indistinctly seen couched on their plaids, in the more remote recesses of the cavern.

Waverley, 17

Torches: and we are told what material they are made of; what kind of light they produce (qualified by two distinct adjectives); what kind of odor (again qualified by an adjective, which is further qualified in its turn). In this careful sequence of causes and effects, metaphors have been completely ousted by analytical predicates.

---

[24] Here are two more instances, drawn from Hugo's urban historical novel (cities have borders, too, as the next chapter will show): 'The poor poet cast his eyes around him. He was actually in that dreaded Cour des Miracles, into which no honest man had ever penetrated at such an hour, a magic circle [. . .] a hideous wen on the face of Paris; a sewer disgorging every morning and receiving every night that fetid torrent of vice, mendacity, and roguery which always overflows the streets of great capitals; a monstrous hive to which all the drones of the social order retired at night with their booty; the hospital of imposture . . .' (*Notre Dame de Paris*, II.6). And later, at the opposite pole of Paris: 'It is certain, moreover, that the archdeacon was smitten with a strange passion for the symbolic porch of Notre Dame, that page of conjuration written in stone [. . .] for its signification, for its myth, for its hidden meaning, for the symbol concealed beneath the sculptures of its facade, like a first text under the second of a palympsest – in short, for the enigma which it incessantly proposes to the understanding' (*Notre Dame de Paris*, IV.4).

The description is not 'objective', of course (none ever is), but internal, expository: instead of the emotional impact with an unknown reality, its form is that of detailed articulation.

It is an instance of what Ernest Gellner has (metaphorically) called 'single intellectual currency':

> By the common or single intellectual currency I mean that all facts are located within a single continuous logical space [. . .], and so that in principle one single language describes the world and is internally unitary; or on the negative side, that there are no special, privileged, insulated facts or realms, protected from contamination or contradiction by others, and living in insulated independent spaces of their own. Just this was, of course, the most striking trait of pre-modern, pre-rational visions: the coexistence within them of multiple, not properly united, but hierarchically related sub-worlds, and the existence of special privileged facts, sacralized and exempt from ordinary treatment.[25]

A continuous logical space: like the analytical dominant of Scott's second description. And note Gellner's own extended metaphor: society as a system of language-spaces – *which are being forced open*. State-building requires streamlining, I said earlier: of physical barriers, and of the many jargons and dialects that are irreversibly reduced to a single national language. And the style of nineteenth-century novels – informal, impersonal, 'common' – contributes to this centralization more than any other discourse. In this, too, the novel is truly the symbolic form of the nation-state.[26]

Near the border, figurality goes up. Beyond the border, it subsides. Geography does indeed act upon style, in historical novels. And in other novels?

In other novels, yes and no. Yes, because there too style changes according to space. But no, because it changes with *space* – not with

---

[25] Ernest Gellner, *Nations and Nationalism*, Cornell University Press, Ithaca 1983, p. 21.

[26] In general, the novel has not stimulated social polyphony (as Bakhtin would have it), but rather reduced it (as I have tried to show here and there in *The Way of the World* and *Modern Epic*). The undeniable polyphony of the Russian novel of ideas is in this respect the exception, not the rule, of novelistic evolution: not by chance generated, as we have seen in figure 11, by a *European*, not a national frame.

geography. Although metaphors still increase near the border, the latter is only seldom a geographical entity: usually, it belongs to a scale of experience for which the term 'geography' is wholly inappropriate. The staircase of the Gothic, the window in *Wuthering Heights*, the threshold in Dostoevsky, the pit in *Germinal*: here are some 'frontiers' of great metaphorical intensity – none of which is however a geographical border.

But there is more. As style is indeed correlated to space, so *space is correlated to plot*: from Propp to Lotman, the crossing of a spatial border is usually also the decisive event of the narrative structure. The relationship, here, is a triangular one: tropes, space, and plot. And the triangle poses a further question. Tropes increase near the border, fine. But why?

It is not easy to find answers in the existing theories of metaphor, because they usually focus on 'what' a metaphor is – whereas I am asking 'when' it is, or 'where'. *The Rule of Metaphor*, however, in a chapter on 'the intersection of the spheres of discourse' (another spatial metaphor . . .), offers a promising beginning. Metaphors become indispensable, Ricœur writes, when we must 'explore a referential field that is not directly accessible'; and he goes on:

> The second meaning [. . .] relates to a referential field for which there is no direct characterization, for which we consequently are unable to make identifying descriptions by means of appropriate predicates.
>
> Unable to fall back upon the interplay between reference and predication, the semantic aim has recourse to a network of predicates that already function in a familiar field of reference. This already constituted meaning is raised from its anchorage in an initial field of reference and cast into the new referential field which it will then work to delineate.[27]

A *network* raised from its *anchorage* and *cast* into a new *field* . . . Like Waverley, or Pierre Gringoire, Ricœur finds himself in uncharted territory, and uses one metaphor after another (including Novalis' wonderful one – 'theories are nets: only he who casts will catch' – that forms the epigraph of Popper's *Logic of Scientific*

[27] Paul Ricœur, *The Rule of Metaphor*, 1975, Toronto University Press, 1979, pp. 298-9.

Discovery). And this is indeed the point: in an unknown space, we need an immediate 'semantic sketch' of our surroundings (Ricœur again), *and only metaphors know how to do it*. Only metaphors, I mean, can simultaneously *express* the unknown we must face, and yet also *contain* it. They express it, they 'say' it, via the strangeness of their predication – demons in a monster's jaws, court of miracles, palimpsest of stone – that sounds like a sort of alarm bell (something is very baffling, here). But since metaphors use a 'familiar field of reference', they also *give form* to the unknown: they contain it, and keep it somehow under control.[28]

This is why metaphors are so frequent near the border, then – and so *in*frequent, by contrast, once the latter is passed. Beyond the border, they are no longer indispensable: they can be replaced by analytical, 'appropriate' predicates. And since most novels spend most of their time inside this or that space, rather than on the border between them, it becomes equally clear why metaphors play in novels such a marginal role. I was taught to read novels, a Cambridge student once told me, by turning the pages, and waiting for the damned metaphors. And they never, ever showed up.

7. *Taking the high road*

Jane Austen, and the 'core' of the nation-state. Historical novels, and borders. In the next chapter, urban novels (and in the next book, who knows, regional ones). The novel and the nation-state, reads this

---

[28] Following Ricœur, I am confining myself to the cognitive role of metaphors: but their *emotional* function is clearly just as relevant (after all, describing people like demons, or alleys like sewers, is hardly a passionless sketch). The point was unforgettably made by Arnaud and Nicole in the *Logique de Port-Royal*: 'Figural expressions signify, besides the main thing, the movement and passion of the speaker, and impress therefore on our spirit the one and the other, whereas simple expressions indicate the naked truth only' (Antoine Arnaud and Pierre Nicole, *La Logique ou l'art de penser*, 1662–83, part one, chapter 14). The emotional function of metaphor is itself closely correlated to space: on the brink of an unknown field, our semantic sketch must suggest not only what the unknown is – but what it is *for us*. 'We don't judge things for what they are in themselves', write Arnaud and Nicole, 'but for what they are in respect to us: and truth and utility are for us one and the same thing' (ibid., part three, chapter 20).

chapter's title: and it's like putting together a puzzle, one piece, one space at a time. And now, with a leap backwards to the very beginning of the modern European novel – roads (figure 17).

Everything was sliding South, writes Pierre Chaunu of sixteenth-century Spain, and the picaresque certainly agrees. Castile works here as a sort of large funnel, that, between Salamanca and Alcalà de Henares, collects all the main characters and channels them towards Madrid, Toledo, Sevilla (while minor figures sketch out Spain's periphery: Leon, Asturias, Biscayne, Aragon . . .). These novels turn their back to the pilgrims of the *Camino de Santiago* for roads that are much more worldly, and crowded, and wealthy. 'The victory of the mule, in the sixteenth century, is undeniable', writes Braudel in *The Mediterranean*;[29] true, and with this modest and stubborn animal – which is also, remember, Sancho Panza's best friend – European narrative changes forever. Mules against ships, one could say (and against aristocratic steeds): the wonder of the open sea, with its extraordinary adventures, is replaced by a slow and regular progress; daily, tiresome, often banal. *But such is precisely the secret of the modern novel* (of 'realism', if you wish): modest episodes, with a limited narrative value – and yet, never without *some* kind of value. At the beginning of *Guzmán de Alfarache*, in the first fifteen miles, we read of three inns, two encounters along the road (a mule-driver, two priests), a case of mistaken identity, two interventions by the guards, and three swindles. In fifteen miles . . .

On the roads, mules; and at regular intervals (the 15–20 miles of a day's journey), inns: where one can find work, sex, gambling, food, religion, petty crime, entertainment. All parts of picaresque Spain thus end up resembling each other (everywhere mule-drivers, innkeepers, guards, priests, whores, young squires, gamblers, thieves . . .); but they are also always a little different, because the dozen basic characters are reshuffled at every new stop, their combinations change, and the novel can go on without losing interest. And then, the regularity of the pattern is enlivened by the stories one hears on

[29] Braudel, *The Mediterranean*, p. 284.

17. Spanish picaresque novels during the sixteenth and seventeenth centuries

The width of the road corresponds to the frequency with which the picaros travel on it. The map also includes the journey of Don Quixote (DQ), who is however looking for chivalric adventures, and therefore never comes close to the prosaic, well-trodden roads of the picaresque. *La picara Justina*, which is the only one of these novels to have a female protagonist, is confined to a different, smaller space from the rest: spatial limitation which recalls Lucia's short journey in *The Betrothed* (figure 16) and will return in the nineteenth-century European *Bildungsroman* (figure 31).

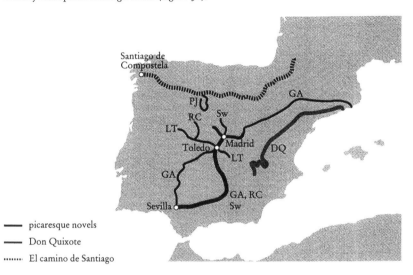

——— picaresque novels

——— Don Quixote

········· El camino de Santiago

Novels included:

GA   Mateo Alemán *Guzmán de Alfarache*, I and II
LT   anonymous *Lazarillo da Tormes*
PJ   López de Ubeda *La picara Justina*
RC   Miguel de Cervantes *Rinconete y Cortadilo*
Sw   Francisco de Quevedo *The Swindler*

Encounters in a novel usually take place 'on the road'. The road is a particularly good place for random encounters. On the road ('the high road'), the spatial and temporal paths of the most varied people – representatives of all social classes, estates, religions, nationalities, ages – intersect at one spatial and temporal point. People who are normally kept separate by social and spatial distance can accidentally meet; any contrast may crop up, the most varied fates may collide and interweave with one another.

MIKHAIL BAKHTIN, *Forms of Time and of the Chronotope in the Novel*

the road, and the swindles that occur along it, in a narrative system that needs very little fuel to spin out its plots. It's the formula of modern success: low cost, and reliable output.

A country of roads: where strangers meet, walk together, tell each other the story of their lives, drink from the same flask, share the

---

18. *Gil Blas*

As the map indicates, most of the first encounters occur on the road, or in very small towns, while characters run into each other again in a handful of large cities – Valencia, Granada, Madrid – which appear thus as veritable concentrates of the Spanish nation. As a certain amount of time always elapses between first and second encounters, and the mere fact of seeing someone again encourages long narratives of the intervening years, the map supports Benedict Anderson's intuition that the novel may be seen as 'a complex gloss on the word "meanwhile"'.

○ first encounter

● later encounter

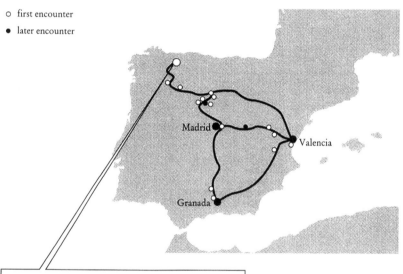

And here I am, just outside Oviedo, on the Peñaflor road, surrounded by the countryside; my own master, and the master of a bad mule as well, forty ducats, and a few reales stolen from my honoured uncle. First of all, I let go of the reins, allowing the mule to do whatever she pleased . . .

ALAIN-RENÉ LESAGE, *Gil Blas*, I.2

same bed . . . It's the great symbolic achievement of the picaresque: defining the modern nation as that space where strangers are never entirely strangers – and at any rate don't remain so for long. In *Gil Blas*, a late classic of the genre, the hero's long tour of Spain becomes a veritable relay race, where characters meet and drift apart, meet again, separate again – but always without great emotions (figure 18). Unlike classical agnitions, Lesage's re-encounters are never dramatic: no dying fathers, or girls abducted from their cradle; just friends, or fellow travelers, or occasional lovers. This network of pleasant, unproblematic episodes, defines the nation as the new space of 'familiarity', where human beings re-cognize each other as members of the same wide group. Serenely, and without tragedies.

Tragedies occur elsewhere, as in the interpolated narratives of figure 19. There is plenty of Spain, here too: but tilted towards the coast (and towards Portugal); and then the Mediterranean, North Africa, Italy, Greece, three or four islands, a half-dozen ports . . . This much wider scenario is still ruled – after fifteen centuries! – by the

---

19. Lesage's Mediterranean

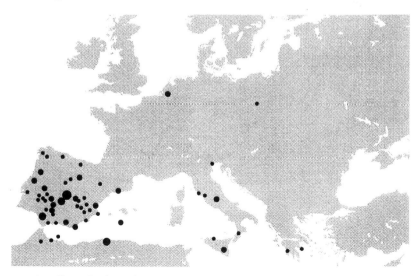

● setting of interpolated narratives

conventions of Hellenistic romances (figure 20): it's a world of storms and shipwrecks; of wars, betrayals, death. Of personal insecurity, especially: where one may be easily enslaved by the enemy – and the freedom of small daily choices, which is so typical of the picaresque road, is crushed by the power of the past.

---

20. The geographical setting of Hellenistic novels

A map of the Mediterranean region showing the routes of the hero and heroine of a novel inevitably brings to mind the school-bible's map of the travels of St Paul. Here Xenophon's *Ephesian Tale* is mapped. The continuous line (——) indicates the hero and heroine's journey together from Ephesus via Samos and Rhodes to somewhere in the middle of the sea, where their ship is attacked by pirates. From the pirates' headquarters in Tyre the heroine (dotted line: ·······) is taken to Antioch, sold to slave-traders, shipwrecked off the Cilician coast, saved at the last moment from a new marriage in Tarsus, brought back to Alexandria, to Memphis, and up the Nile to the Ethiopian border; then back to Alexandria, and across the sea to a brothel in Tarentum. Meanwhile, the hero (broken line: – – –) is searching desperately for her, sometimes close on her heels, sometimes going totally astray. At last they are reunited on Rhodes and return home to Ephesus.

THOMAS HÄGG, *The Novel in Antiquity*

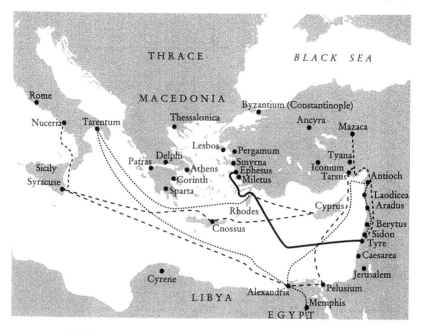

——— route of the hero and heroine together   ········ route of the heroine   – – – route of the hero

The novel and the nation-state. So be it. But Lesage's 'Mediter-ranean' interpolations show that their meeting was far from inevitable. The novel didn't simply find the nation as an obvious, pre-formed fictional space: it had to wrest it from other geographical matrixes that were just as capable of generating narrative – and that indeed clashed with each other throughout the eighteenth century.

---

21. Geographical setting of French novels 1750–1800

In the second half of the eighteenth century, the narrative role of France and Europe remains roughly the same, while that of Britain doubles, and that of non-European countries slightly decreases. The most radical change however concerns imaginary and utopian settings, which in fifty years decline from 13 to 2 percent. Taken together, narratives located in France and Britain rise from 45 percent (in 1751–60) to 58 percent (1791–1800), and those located in Europe from 68 to 85 percent: two signs of the progressive contraction of novelistic geography.

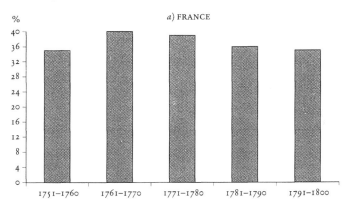

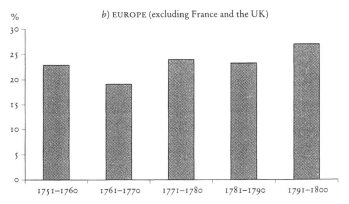

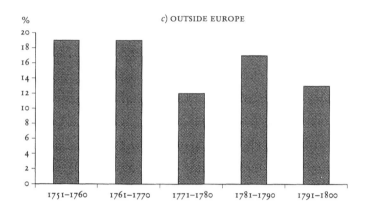

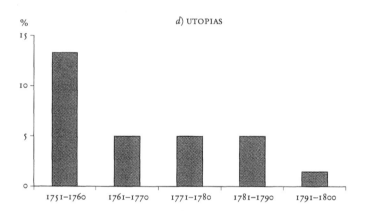

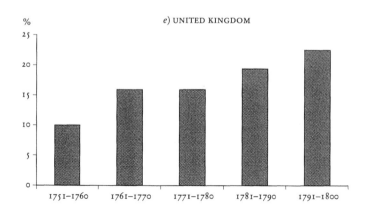

At one extreme, supra-national genres, like the *Robinsonades*, or the *contes philosophiques*; at the opposite one, local love stories, like *Pamela*, or *Werther*; and in an intermediate, national/cosmopolitan position, most other texts – including, say, *Moll Flanders, Manon Lescaut, Wilhelm Meister,* and *Gil Blas* itself. According to Angus Martin's research on the French novel, these different spatial options more or less balance each other for quite a long time, and it is only at the very end of the century that the contraction of narrative space becomes finally visible (figure 21).

Visible, in the novel. But short narratives remain largely indifferent to the new symbolic geography, and *Gil Blas'* internal asymmetry ('Spanish' novel, and 'Mediterranean' tales) reappears in the pages of a famous periodical of the late eighteenth century, *The Lady's Magazine*: here, novels are set almost entirely in Europe (Britain, France, Germany, Italy, Hungary), whereas short stories and 'anecdotes' are often located in the Middle East, India, China,

22. *The Lady's Magazine* 1798–1802, serialized novels

- 1–30 columns
- over 80 columns

23. *The Lady's Magazine* 1798–1802, short narratives

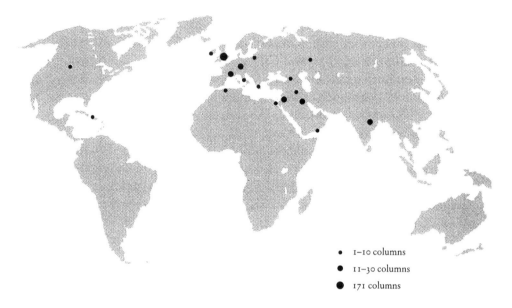

• 1–10 columns
● 11–30 columns
● 171 columns

24. *The Lady's Magazine* 1798–1802, anecdotes

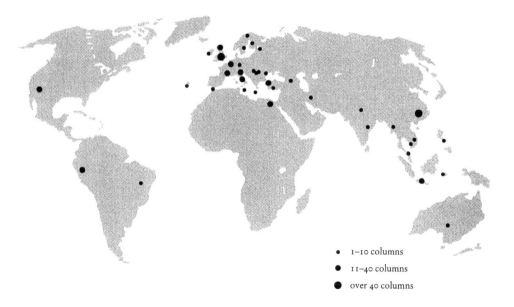

• 1–10 columns
● 11–40 columns
● over 40 columns

the Americas (figures 22–24).[30] As always, morphology is a powerful reason for fictional geography: the novel leans towards the representation of the everyday, and prefers a nearby, well-known reality; short narratives thrive on the strange, the 'unheard-of' (Goethe), and are quite at ease in remote and fabulous lands, where a total lack of genuine information (figure 25) places no fetters on the imagination. And then, this eastward drift is a long-term effect, a late homage to Indian and Arabic culture, and their formative influence on European short stories. I will return to this in the third chapter.

[30] The 171 columns located in Britain in figure 23 (usually, in an unspecified 'countryside') are a glaring exception to the pattern just outlined. Almost all of them are uncomplicated sentimental stories (love at first sight, childhood love rekindled in youth, happiness restored by proximity to nature, etc.), and I wonder whether these narrative materials may have anything to do with the geographical setting.

25. *The Lady's Magazine* 1798–1802, 'foreign news'

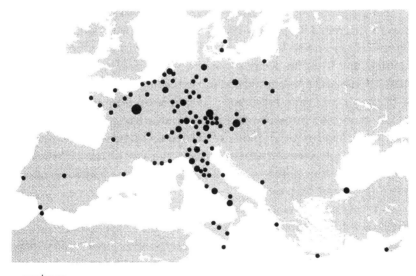

not shown:
- Alexandria
- Stockholm
- San Domingo
- Egypt
- Petersburg
- Philadelphia

- 1–5 mentions
- 6–20 mentions
- 21–40 mentions
- 82 mentions

8. 'A mighty big river, resembling an immense snake uncoiled'

The picaresque: roads that intersect, branch off, converge on Toledo or Sevilla. But outside Europe the shape of the journey changes abruptly, as for instance in the colonial romances of figure 26. This is a familiar image, for most Europeans: a map of exploration journeys, *tel quel*. The starting point is the same: a port, a garrison, a trading station along the coast: one of those 'rim settlements', as the geography of colonialism calls them, from which European conquest began. The endpoint is also the same: an isolated site in the interior of Africa, disconnected from every other route, on the border of the unknown (Conrad's 'blank spaces on the earth'), or of uninhabitable lands (the forest, the desert). And finally, the 'shape' of the journey is the same: the single, one-dimensional line that has been the standard sign of African explorations in map after map.

An isolated line, with no deviations, no lateral branches. Of the novels discussed so far, not one could be visualized in such a way. From Longbourn to Pemberley, Elizabeth's road is far from simple: it implicates London, Kent, a journey (just missed) to the Lake District; Elizabeth herself could end up on the 'lateral' branch of the plot – Brighton, and then Newcastle, in exile with Wickham. Waverley could easily find himself with Prince Charlie (who is buried in a big ugly church in Frascati), and Gil Blas end up lost at sea, like so many in Lesage; and as for the urban novels of the next chapter, the multiplicity of possible paths – of crossroads, and bifurcations – is one of their distinctive features.

But colonial romances have no bifurcations. No well-lit inns, or brilliant officers, or picturesque castles that may induce one to wander from the prescribed path. In these stories – as in their archetypal image: the expedition that moves slowly, in single file, towards the horizon – there is only a linear movement: forwards, or backwards. There are no deviations, no *alternatives* to the pre-scribed path, but only obstacles – and therefore, antagonists. Friends, and foes. On one side the white men, their guide, Western technology, a discolored old map. On the other...

26. Colonial romances

...... British novels
—— French novels

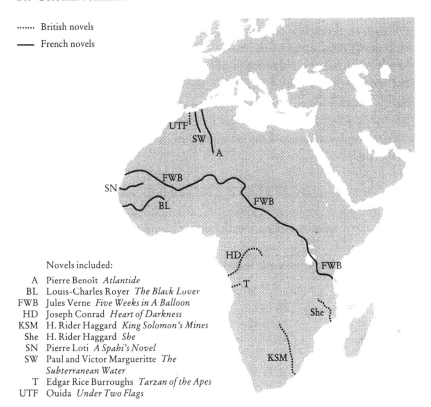

Novels included:

A Pierre Benoît *Atlantide*
BL Louis-Charles Royer *The Black Lover*
FWB Jules Verne *Five Weeks in A Balloon*
HD Joseph Conrad *Heart of Darkness*
KSM H. Rider Haggard *King Solomon's Mines*
She H. Rider Haggard *She*
SN Pierre Loti *A Spahi's Novel*
SW Paul and Victor Margueritte *The Subterranean Water*
T Edgar Rice Burroughs *Tarzan of the Apes*
UTF Ouida *Under Two Flags*

Now when I was a little chap I had a passion for maps [...] At that time there were many blank spaces on the earth, and when I saw one that looked particularly inviting on a map (but they all look that) I would put my finger on it and say, When I grow up I will go there [...] I have been in some of them, and ... well, we won't talk about that. But there was one yet – the biggest, the most blank, so to speak – that I had a hankering after [...] there was in it one river especially, a mighty big river, that you could see on the map, resembling an immense snake uncoiled, with its head in the sea, its body at rest curving afar over a vast country, and its tail lost in the depths of the land. And as I looked at the map of it in a shop-window, it fascinated me as a snake would a bird – a silly little bird.

JOSEPH CONRAD, *Heart of Darkness*

On the other lions, heat, vegetation, elephants, flies, rain, illness – and natives. All mixed up, and at bottom all interchangeable in their function as obstacles: all equally unknowable and threatening. Contemptuous confusion of the natural and the human, which conveys the ultimate message of colonial romances: Africans are animals. The text wouldn't even need to *say* so (although it almost always does, even Conrad): the linear plot is such a strong modelization of space that readers cannot but 'see' these human beings as a race of (dangerous) beasts. Ideology and narrative matrix, here, are truly one and the same.

A linear narrative. But how did it come into being? The three diagrams of figure 27 suggest a possible answer. The European experience of African space begins with 'rim settlements' (phase A), which

27. An ideal-typical sequence of transport-system development

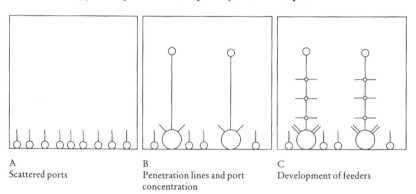

A
Scattered ports

B
Penetration lines and port concentration

C
Development of feeders

Sometimes we came upon a station close by the bank, clinging to the skirts of the unknown, and the whitemen rushing out of a tumbledown hovel, with great gestures of joy and surprise and welcome, seemed very strange – had the appearance of being held there captive by a spell. The word ivory would ring in the air for a while – and on we went again into the silence, along empty reaches, round the still bends, between the high walls of our winding way [. . .] At night sometimes the roll of drums behind the curtain of trees would run up the river and remain sustained faintly . . .

JOSEPH CONRAD, *Heart of Darkness*

are then quickly linked (phase B) to those inland areas that are rich in those raw materials (including human beings) that the colonial power is eager to obtain. And, basically, this is it. A colonial regime may reach the next phase (C: development of lateral 'feeders' along the main line), but hardly much more. Colonialism aims at re-directing the local economy *outwards*: towards the sea, the metropolis, the world market. A good internal distribution is literally none of its business.

If colonial romances show such geographically one-dimensional plots, then, the reason is not that Africa lacks a system of roads; not at all, roads have existed there for centuries (figure 28). But this network does not serve European *interests*, and so it also eludes the

---

28. The trans-Saharian routes

Notice how this intricate trading system has no equivalent in the colonial romances of figure 26 set in the same area (*Under Two Flags, The Subterranean Water, Atlantide*).

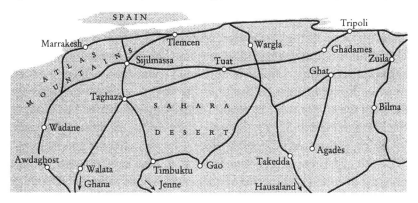

Muslims crossed the Sahara as merchants and travellers with the caravans of camels that regularly made the hazardous journey from the trading depots on either edge of the desert, such as Sijilmassa, south of the Atlas mountains in Morocco, and Walata in Mali. This dangerous trade carried luxury goods (and in time firearms) and salt – a vital element in the diet in tropical countries – to the black African lands south of the Sahara. In exchange, gold, leather-work and slaves went northwards.

GEOFFREY BARRACLOUGH, ed., *The Times Atlas of World History*

European *perception* of Africa. And worse. Before 1800, write Knox and Agnew, Africa possesses a 'pre-colonial spatial structure [. . .] of inter-regional trading networks'. But after that date, and especially after 1880,

> these networks are disrupted as capitalist penetration from the coasts reoriented regional economies to long-distance external ties. The older inter-regional networks were dissolved both by the imposition of new political boundaries that bore little relationship to them and by the construction of railways to service new plantations, mining concerns and settler estates.[31]

Penetrate; seize; leave (and if needed, destroy). It's the spatial logic of colonialism; duplicated, and 'naturalized', by the spatial logic of the one-dimensional plot. And then, at the end of the journey (with the exception of *Heart of Darkness*), we don't find raw materials, or ivory, or human beings to be enslaved. In lieu of these prosaic realities, a fairy-tale entity – a 'treasure' – where the bloody profits of the colonial adventure are sublimated into an aesthetic, almost self-referential object: glittering, *clean* stones: diamonds, if possible (as in *King Solomon's Mines*). Or else, an enigmatic lover: a sort of jungle Dracula, who in two very popular texts (*She*, *Atlantide*) is actually a supernatural being. Or again, and most typically, at the end of the journey lies the figure of the Lost European, who retrospectively justifies the entire story as a case of legitimate defense. The Congo, the Haggar, central Africa, the land of the Zulus, the Sahara outposts: in this continent teeming with white prisoners that long to be freed, Western conquest can be rewritten as a genuine *liberation*, with a reversal of roles (a 'rhetoric of innocence', I have called it in *Modern Epic*) that is possibly the greatest trick of the colonial imagination.[32]

---

[31] Paul Knox and John Agnew, *The Geography of the World Economy*, 1989, Edward Arnold, London–New York 1994, pp. 84–5.

[32] The search for the Lost European may have been suggested by the Stanley–Livingstone story: perhaps it existed first in reality, and only later in fiction. On the other hand, I suspect that the figure of Livingstone had such an exceptional symbolic appeal because it 're-awakened' a fairy-tale stereotype (Propp's 'abduction into another kingdom': although, of course, Livingstone had not been abducted), transposing it onto African soil. If this is true, then a real event was 'used' by a fictional convention to strengthen its hold on the European imagination.

And innocence – that is, the guilty desire to appear innocent – is what comes to mind in front of figure 29. I found it by chance, in an issue of the *Journal of Geography* for the year 1974 (nineteen-seventy-four), in an article entitled 'A Game of European Colonization in Africa'. As you can see, it is a board game designed as a teaching aid, a sort of 'Monopoly', where the five players ('England, France, Belgium, Germany, Portugal') throw the dice, move, buy the various territories (the most expensive one is the Cape of Good Hope), draw the 'Fate' and 'Fortune' cards (the worst, a 'native

---

29. Playing with Africa

uprising'; the luckiest one, a gift from an 'American philanthropist'). And I will add only this: to win, you must build, not houses and hotels, but schools and hospitals.

9. *Village, provinces, metropolis*

Roads and cities, in the picaresque; roads and cities, in the *Bildungsroman*. But the center of gravity has shifted. In the Spain of Lazarillo and his like, the emphasis is on the road, where life is free and endlessly open, while in towns one ends up as a servant, and with an empty stomach to boot. In the evolution of the *Bildungsroman*, by contrast, the road disappears step by step, and the foreground is occupied by the great capital cities – London, Paris, Petersburg, Madrid... (figure 31). Be careful, my son, entreats the hero's mother in Goncharov's *A Common Story*: 'be careful, now that you are setting forth for a foreign country. . .'. And the son: 'mother, what foreign country? I am going to Petersburg!' Well, for the *Bildungsroman* they are both right: the great city is truly another world, if compared to the rest of the country – but the narrative will bind it once and for all to the provinces, constructing it as the natural goal of all young men of talent. And around the great capitals, a cosmopolitan scenario opens up, where the ambition of the modern *Bildung* – Lydgate, who goes to study pathology in the country of the great Bichat – entwines itself to the aesthetic geography of the Grand Tour: London, Paris, Switzerland, Rome, the Rhine, the Low Countries... (figure 32).

---

30. **The three spaces of the European *Bildungsroman***

village	provinces	capital city
old	–	young
family	–	unknown
–	school, trade, civil service	law, politics, finance, literature, theater, art, journalism
five significant characters	six characters	fifteen characters

It is a new articulation of space, whose most significant elements are charted in figure 30. Age disparity, first of all: old people in the village, and young ones in the city. Asymmetry with a basis in reality, of course (urbanization is mostly for young people), and through which the *Bildungsroman* redefines the non-contemporaneity of European nation-states as a *physiological* fact – leaving behind the pathological tensions of historical novels. Between Angoulême and Paris, or Rochester and London, or Fratta and Venice, the difference is no longer one of civilizations, but of fashions; fashion, this great metropolitan idea, designed for young people (and by them); this engine that never stops, and makes the provinces feel old and ugly and jealous – and seduces them forever and a day.

The old/young opposition overlaps with the following one: family, and strangers. In the village, not only are mothers (or substitute mothers) always present, but every important relationship takes the form of a family tie: early sweethearts are sister figures (Little Emily, Laura in *Pendennis*, Biddy, Pisana, Anna in Keller, Laure in Flaubert), while early friends are as many older brothers (Werner, Fouqué, David Sechard, Deslauriers). In the great city, though, the heroes of the *Bildungsroman* change overnight from 'sons' into 'young men': their affective ties are no longer vertical ones (between successive generations), but horizontal, within the same generation. They are drawn towards those unknown yet congenial faces seen in the gardens, or at the theater; future friends, or rivals, or both, that eye each other from behind newspapers, or pass the bread basket at Flicoteaux – which is the most beautiful place in the world.

It is the universe of 'secondary socialization'; of work, summarized in figure 30's third line. In the provinces, one can be a tutor (Julien Sorel), a tradesman (Wilhelm Meister; Carlo Altoviti), a civil servant (Carlo again; the green Heinrich). In the city, apart from Julien's ancien régime post as secretary of the Marquis de la Mole, the choices are finance (Frédéric Moreau), politics (Pendennis, Frédéric again), the law (Pip, David Copperfield), the theater (Wilhelm Meister), painting (Heinrich), and, of course, journalism and literature

31. The European *Bildungsroman*

Some locations of this map are largely conjectural: Meister's and Serlo's towns (here mapped as Frankfurt and Hamburg) in *Wilhelm Meister*; the city of Heinrich's artistic apprenticeship in *The Green Heinrich* (Frankfurt again); while the ending of *Wilhelm Meister*, and the opening of *A Common Story*, are left completely unspecified. This geographical vagueness may well be related to the utopian component of the *Bildungsroman*, which is particularly marked in Goethe's work.

In the novels taking place in France, Britain, Russia, and Spain (that is, in long-established nation-states), the hero's trajectory towards the capital city is usually very direct; in the German, Swiss, and Italian texts, the lack of a clear national center produces by contrast a sort of irresolute wandering (which is however also a way of 'unifying' a nation that does not exist yet). In these novels (and only here) we also encounter several 'castles'; but these residual signs of the old feudal power have become a mere silly interlude in Goethe, a short-lived dream in Keller, and a childhood memory (later literally razed to the ground) in *Confessions of an Italian*.

Finally, in the two texts written by and about women, the journey to the capital either does not occur (*Jane Eyre*), or plays hardly any role (*Middlemarch*), while isolated estates and local institutions (church, school) acquire a major significance. The asymmetry between the space of the hero and that of the heroine is the same as in figures 16 and 17.

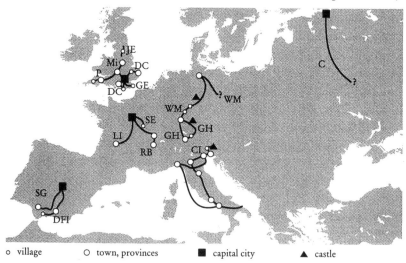

o village   O town, provinces   ■ capital city   ▲ castle

Novels included:

C Ivan Goncharov *A Common Story*
CI Ippolito Nievo *Confessions of an Italian*
DC Charles Dickens *David Copperfield*
DFI Juan Valera *Doctor Faustino's Illusions*
GE Charles Dickens *Great Expectations*
GH Gottfried Keller *The Green Heinrich*
JE Charlotte Brontë *Jane Eyre*
LI Honoré de Balzac *Lost Illusions*
Mi George Eliot *Middlemarch*

P William Thackeray *The History of Pendennis*
RB Stendhal *The Red and the Black*
SE Gustave Flaubert *Sentimental Education*
SG Gomez de Bedoya *The School of the Great World*
WM Wolfgang Goethe *Wilhelm Meister's Apprenticeship*

32. The international scenario of the European *Bildungsroman*

Where the symbolic role of the national capital is strongest (as in France), travels abroad have a peripheral function (*The Red and the Black*, *Sentimental Education*), or are completely absent (*Lost Illusions*). By contrast, foreign journeys play a major role in *The School of the Great World*, *Confessions of an Italian*, and especially in *Middlemarch*, where the encounter with Europe transforms in depth the three central characters, making them impatient with the narrowess of provincial life. On the other hand, the protagonists of the *Bildungsroman* seldom embark on long-distance journeys, and travel outside of Europe is usually left to their alter egos (Lothario, Judith, St. John Rivers). The only exceptions are Pip (who, however, is following in a friend's footsteps, and returns to England for the novel's ending), and Frédéric Moreau (but it's not clear whether he actually leaves Europe; and anyway, he goes as a tourist, and is back in three lines). The *Bildungsroman*'s reluctance to leave the old world was expressed once and for all by Goethe, in Lothario's famous words about the German countryside: 'Here, or nowhere, is America!'

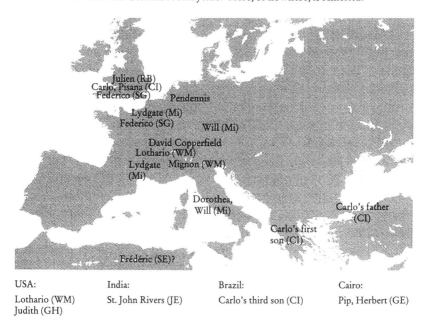

USA:

Lothario (WM)
Judith (GH)

India:

St. John Rivers (JE)

Brazil:

Carlo's third son (CI)

Cairo:

Pip, Herbert (GE)

Novels included:

CI   Ippolito Nievo *Confessions of an Italian*
DC   Charles Dickens *David Copperfield*
GE   Charles Dickens *Great Expectations*
GH   Gottfried Keller *The Green Heinrich*
JE   Charlotte Brontë *Jane Eyre*
LI   Honoré de Balzac *Lost Illusions*
Mi   George Eliot *Middlemarch*
P   William Thackeray *The History of Pendennis*

RB   Stendhal *The Red and the Black*
SE   Gustave Flaubert *Sentimental Education*
SG   Gomez de Bedoya *The School of the Great World*
WM   Wolfgang Goethe *Wilhelm Meister's Apprenticeship*

(Federico in the *The School of the Great World*, Lucien de Rubem-pré, David Copperfield, Pendennis, Doctor Faustino).[33] *Lost Illusions*, at bottom, says it all: to the provinces the endless, heavy task of physically producing paper; to the capital, the privilege of covering those beautiful white sheets with fascinating ideas (and glittering nonsense). The division of labor that only a great city can afford gives wings to the imagination, encouraging an inventiveness that affects even bourgeois careers, and finds its greatest expression in the passionate discussions of metropolitan youth: Wilhelm's analysis of *Hamlet*, Lucien's journalism 'lessons', Heinrich's painterly strategies, Pendennis' political philosophy ...

These discussions, with their numerous participants, develop in that public sphere where the hero of the *Bildungsroman* must prove himself. The last line of figure 30 tries to indicate this new crowded milieu by charting the number of significant characters present in the various narrative spaces; and mind you, the difference between five and fifteen is not just a matter of quantity, here: it's a qualitative, morphological one. With five characters (a mother, a son, and usually a sister-beloved, and a brother-best friend), the plot is usually confined within one social group, and slides towards two opposite, but equally stable arrangements: idyllic peace (Keller, Nievo, Goncharov, early sections of *Meister*, *The Red and the Black*, *Great Expectations*), or unbearable despotism (Verrières' 'public opinion', Mr Murdstone, Mrs Reed, the monopoly of the Cointet brothers). With ten or twenty characters, on the other hand, it is possible, and in fact inevitable, to include in the sociological spectrum distant, and openly hostile groups. The narrative system becomes complicated, unstable: the city turns into a gigantic roulette table, where helpers and antagonists mix in unpredictable combinations, in a game that remains open for a very long time, and has many possible outcomes

---

[33] The heroes' alter egos strengthen the pattern: plenty of tradesmen in the provinces, and intellectuals in cities. Significantly enough, manual labour is absent from both spaces: a tacit acknowledgment of the fact that, in a capitalist society, manual labour does not contribute to the formation of a fully developed human being, but rather to his or her disintegration – as *Jude the Obscure* will make clear at the end of the century.

(figure 33). Quantity has produced a new form: the novel of complexity. This will be the topic of the next chapter.

---

33. *Lost Illusions*

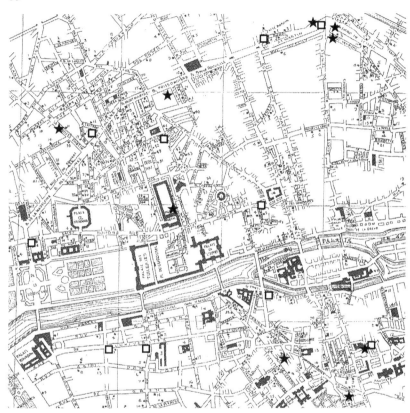

★ Lucien's helpers
☐ Lucien's antagonists

'Well now, my dear friend', said Finot to Des Lupeaulx, 'tell me the truth. Is Lucien getting serious patronage? He has become the bête noire of all my staff; and before supporting them in their conspiracy, I wanted to consult you in order to know whether it would be better to foil it and serve him.'

'My friend', said Des Lupeaulx, 'how can you imagine that the Marquise d'Espard, Châtelet and Madame de Bargeton, who has had the Baron appointed Prefect of the Charante and made a Count as a preparation for their triumphal return to Angoulême, have forgiven Lucien for his attacks? They have thrown him into the royalist party in order to eliminate him.'

HONORÉ DE BALZAC, *Lost Illusions*, II.37

10. *Theoretical interlude II. Geography of plot*

Maps; spatial patterns: granted. But are we sure that they are indeed conveyed to readers, and that readers find them significant? Character X lives in Dorset, Y and Z in Kent, they all meet at Bath, fine: but can't one simply forget all these references, given how inconspicuous they often are? Shouldn't we extend Bakhtin's skepticism about Greek romances to all narrative geography?

> The nature of a given place does not figure as a component of the event; the place figures solely as a naked, abstract expanse of space. All adventures in the Greek romance are thus governed by an interchangeability of space; what happens in Babylon could just as well happen in Egypt or Byzantium and viceversa.[34]

Readers will judge, of course, but I hope to have shown that what happens in the Highlands could *not* 'just as well happen' in the Home Counties or viceversa; and that, by the same token, 'the nature of a given place' (Lesage's road, Pushkin's border, or Conrad's river) *is* indeed 'a component of the event': in the sense that *each space determines, or at least encourages, its own kind of story*. There is no picaresque of the border, or *Bildungsroman* of the European in Africa: *this* specific form needs *that* specific space – the road, the metropolis. Space is not the 'outside' of narrative, then, but an internal force, that shapes it from within. Or in other words: in modern European novels, *what* happens depends a lot on *where* it happens. And so, whether we know it or not – we do so many things, without knowing that we are doing them – by following 'what happens' we come up with a mental map of the many 'wheres' of which our world is made.

What happens depends on where it happens . . . It could be the slogan of Bakhtin's chronotope, and of the book that provided its latent theoretical scaffold: Vladimir Propp's *Morphology of the Folktale*. Figure 34 highlights precisely the spatial foundation of Propp's

---

[34] Bakhtin, 'Forms of Time', p. 100.

narratology: the fact that all of his thirty-one functions *can only occur within specific spaces*. The first eleven, for instance, can only happen in the 'initial world'; the following three, in the space of the donor; then five in the 'other kingdom', three more or less on the border, and the final nine again in the initial world.

One cannot have, say, 'villainy' in the space of the donor, or 'struggle' in the initial world: each function is *ortgebunden*, bound to its space. And more: space is often literally *written* into the function by Propp's definitions: absentation (the very first one), reconnaissance (the villain's first move), departure (the hero's first move), spatial transference, return, unrecognized arrival . . . And notice how space is emphasized *in the most significant functions*, those that open or close a major plot sequence; including, of course,

---

34. Vladimir Propp, *Morphology of the Folktale*: topography of narrative functions

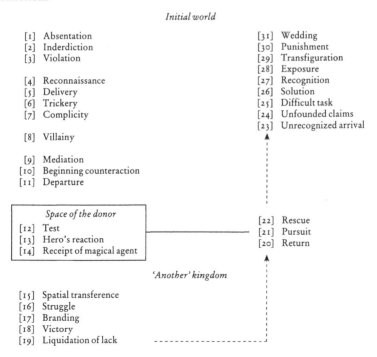

Initial world

[1] Absentation
[2] Inderdiction
[3] Violation

[4] Reconnaissance
[5] Delivery
[6] Trickery
[7] Complicity

[8] Villainy

[9] Mediation
[10] Beginning counteraction
[11] Departure

Space of the donor
[12] Test
[13] Hero's reaction
[14] Receipt of magical agent

'Another' kingdom

[15] Spatial transference
[16] Struggle
[17] Branding
[18] Victory
[19] Liquidation of lack

[31] Wedding
[30] Punishment
[29] Transfiguration
[28] Exposure
[27] Recognition
[26] Solution
[25] Difficult task
[24] Unfounded claims
[23] Unrecognized arrival

[22] Rescue
[21] Pursuit
[20] Return

the *Morphology*'s key function of 'villainy', whose detailed analysis is almost entirely couched in spatial terms.[35]

Morphology of the Folktale ... *topography* of the Folktale would be just as accurate: two worlds, a buffer, two symmetrical circular movements ... How elegant this pattern is; how ordered. How much *more* ordered, in fact, than Austen's world, or Scott's, or the cities of Balzac's and Dickens'. And it makes sense, the fairy-tale is an axiological form, and this is why its space has such simple, clear features: to construct an unquestionable polarity, and project it onto the world, is precisely its task. But in our disenchanted age, this is no longer possible: knowledge has transformed the world from a system of well-marked moral domains into a complicated geography, period. And yet, this very difficulty seems to have induced the novel to its most ambitious wager: to be the bridge between the old and the new, forging a symbolic compromise *between the indifferent world of modern knowledge, and the enchanted topography of magic storytelling*. Between a new geography, that we cannot ignore – and an old narrative matrix, that we cannot forget.

As in all compromises, the success of the attempt is inseparable from a certain ambiguity. In the novel, I mean, although the *Morphology*'s geometric elegance doesn't exactly disappear, it is

[35] 'The villain *abducts* a person [...] The villain *seizes or takes away* a magical agent [...] The villain causes *a sudden disappearance* [...] The villain *expels* someone [...] The villain orders someone to be *thrown into the sea* [...] a case of *expulsion* [...] orders her servant to take her husband *away into the forest* [...] The villain *imprisons or detains* someone' (Vladimir Propp, *Morphology of the Folktale*, 1927, Texas University Press, Austin 1968, pp. 31–4: all italics are mine). In one way or another, all versions of villainy imply a spatial transference; or to quote Propp again: 'Generally, the object of search is located in "another" or "different" kingdom' (p. 50).

My spatial reading of Propp is very similar to S. Ju. Nekljudov's analysis of the Russian *bylina*: '[In the *bylina*] we notice a rigorous fit between specific situations and events, and specific locations. With respect to the hero, these spaces are functional fields, where one is caught in the conflictual pattern specific to the given *locus* (i.e. to the given spatial unit endowed with narrative relevance)' (S. Ju. Nekljudov, 'Il sistema spaziale nell'intreccio della bylina russa', in Jurii M. Lotman, Boris A. Uspenskii, Clara Strada Janovic, eds, *Ricerche semiotiche. Nuove tendenze delle scienze umane nell'URSS*, Italian translation Einaudi, Torino 1973, pp. 107–8).

somewhat *deformed* by the new narrative logic: the distinction between 'initial' and 'other' kingdom loses much of its clarity – while the intermediate space of the donor, which Propp had so firmly delimited, becomes the largest, most unpredictable part of the story. I am thinking of the road of *Lazarillo*, or *Guzmán de Alfarache*, which eclipses the novel's beginning and ending; of Austen's 'relative distance', with its regular pulse of presence and absence; of the city of the *Bildungsroman*, with the many 'lateral' chances that offer themselves each day to the young hero.

The *Morphology* deformed . . . and by novelties that are all pointing in the same direction: towards an *overcoming of the binary narrative matrix*, and of its axiological rigidity.[36] A new kind of story arises: stories of the world in between; not quite neutral (no story ever is), but more complicated, more indeterminate. Or as the next chapter will call them, *stories of the Third.*

[36] Think of how the France/Britain polarization of figure 10 transforms France from a geographical reality into a purely symbolic realm (Propp's enemy kingdom, indeed). And the same is true of colonial romances, which re-activate Propp's functions – departure, encounter with a donor, testing, arrival in the other kingdom, struggle, rescue, return, chase . . . – almost step by step. (That colonial penetration should take the form of a magic folktale is of course quite another instance of the rhetoric of innocence.)

Chapter 2
A tale of two cities

35. Social classes in London according to Charles Booth (1889)

Booth's color-coding, inscribed at the bottom of the map, runs as follows: '*Black*: Lowest class. Vicious, semi-criminal. *Dark blue*: Very poor, casual. Chronic want. *Light blue*: Poor. 18s. to 21s. a week for a moderate family. *Gray*: Mixed. Some comfortable, others poor. *Pink*: Fairly comfortable. Good ordinary earnings. *Red*: Middle class. Well-to-do. *Gold*: Upper-middle and Upper classes. Wealthy.'

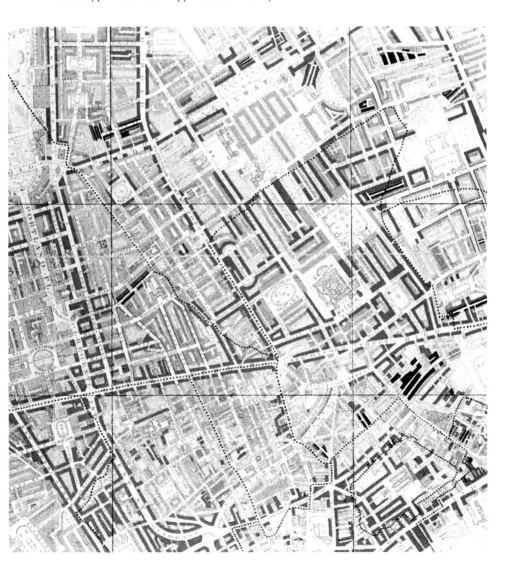

1. *The problem*

Let me begin with a great nineteenth-century map, published in 1889, as the appendix to Charles Booth's *Life and Labour of the People of London* (figure 35). The section shown here (parts of Mayfair, Marylebone, Bloomsbury and Soho) covers only a twentieth of the original, but gives nonetheless a good idea of the work's ambition: a block-by-block investigation of the economic texture of London, with seven colors to stand for seven social groups. Booth's taxonomy is open to question, of course, and his black-to-gold color code is either quite naive or very very ironic. But the facts gathered by his team of researchers are still considered accurate and valuable. So: what does his map show?

At the macroscopic level (which here unfortunately cannot be reproduced), it shows several recurring patterns. Large commercial arteries, for instance – Tottenham Court Road, New Oxford Street, the Strand – trace a bright red network almost everywhere in the city. Extreme poverty peaks near the Thames, and slowly decreases in the direction of the suburbs. Great wealth concentrates in the West End, as always. And so on, and so on.

At the macroscopic level, then, Booth's London is a self-organizing system, with a significant set of regular patterns. At the *micro*scopic level, however, things are different. Take Little Russell Street, just south of the British Museum: lower middle class, the color suggests, but 'fairly comfortable'. South of there, along Bury Street, two or three blocks that are much better-off; but then, just across Oxford Street, a solid black zone: 'vicious, semi-criminal'. Two hundred meters – and three different classes. Heading north, the same two hundred meters would land us in the brilliant gold of Russell Square and Montague Place; heading east, in a working-class area with patches of chronic unemployment and misery. And the same thing would happen in most parts of this map. George Bernard Shaw's residence in 'well-to-do' Fitzroy Square (a few years later, it will be Virginia Woolf's) is surrounded by two rings of 'poor' or 'mixed' streets; in a few blocks, to the north of the Euston Road, workers give way to the 'dangerous classes';[1] to the south, the social fabric rises slowly (and irregularly) towards the middle class; to the west, it turns quickly into élite residences; to the east, it oscillates for quite a long time from one extreme to the other. (And as for Verso's offices, they are in a rather bleak part of Soho: but a good walker could cross the entire spectrum of Booth's seven classes in no more than five minutes.)

What does Booth's map show, then? Two very different things: that the whole is quite ordered – but its individual parts are instead largely random. It is striking how rapid the transitions are, between the urban sub-systems; how poverty replaces wealth at every unpredictable turn of the street (and all this, notwithstanding decades of urban segregation, during which 'an immense geographical gulf had grown up between the rich and the poor of London'[2]). It is the *confusion* evoked with fear and wonder by most London visitors; and confusion, in cities, is always a problem – especially for those in the middle. 'In the city setting', writes Kevin Lynch, 'legibility is crucial':[3] and this London is really not easy to read. Whence the question that this chapter will try to address: given the over-complication

---

[1] 'When Virginia and Adrian moved to Fitzroy Square, Virginia wrote to a friend: "Beatrice comes round, inarticulate with meaning, and begs me not to take the house because of the neighbourhood." She sought the advice of the police, who apparently reassured her' (David Daiches, *Literary Landscapes of the British Isles. A Narrative Atlas*, Facts on File, New York 1980, p. 74).

[2] Gareth Stedman Jones, *Outcast London*, 1971, Penguin, Harmondsworth 1984, p. 247.

[3] Kevin Lynch, *The Image of the City*, MIT Press, Cambridge Mass. 1960, p. 3.

of the nineteenth-century urban setting – how did novels 'read' cities? By what narrative mechanisms did they make them 'legible', and turn urban noise into information?

2. *'We live in so different a part of town . . .'*

One of the first attempts to make London legible was by a genre now largely forgotten: the 'fashionable', or 'silver-fork' novels published by Colburn with enormous success between the mid 1820s and the mid 1840s. So Young Park, at Columbia, has traced the main sites of ten such novels (figure 36); to her map, I have here added one for Bulwer-Lytton's very popular *Pelham* (figure 37), and another for Jane Austen's London (figure 38).

Now, all these figures have one thing in common: they don't show 'London', but only a small, monochrome portion of it: the West End. This is not really a city: it's a class. We live in so different a part of town, says Mrs Gardiner in *Pride and Prejudice*:

'We live in so different a part of town, all our connections are so different, and, as you well know, we go out so little, that it is very improbable [Jane and Bingley] should meet at all, unless he really comes to see her.'

'And that is quite impossible; for he is now in the custody of his friend, and Mr Darcy would no more suffer him to call on Jane in such a part of London! My dear aunt, how could you think of it? Mr Darcy may perhaps have heard of such a place as Gracechurch Street, but he would hardly think a month's ablution enough to cleanse him from its impurities.'

Pride and Prejudice, 25

London as the West End, then. The first 'residential' area of the city, where inhabitants don't work (as they do in Gracechurch Street), but quite simply 'live'. In novel after novel, the same features return: the squares (a great invention of London real estate speculation – Grosvenor Square, Berkeley, Cavendish, Portman, St. James's . . .); the exclusive gathering places (shops in Bond Street, clubs in St. James's, Almacks' ballroom on Pall Mall); the parks (with a clear preference for St. James's, ennobled by its proximity to the crown, and much scorn for 'the *other* park', as Pelham calls the large, open

36. The London of silver-fork novels 1812–40

Novels included: Charlotte Bury, *Self-Indulgence*; T.H. Lister, *Granby*; Robert Plumer Ward, *Tremaine, or the Man of Refinement*; Benjamin Disraeli, *Vivian Grey*; Edward Bulwer-Lytton, *Pelham*; Catherine Gore, *Mothers and Daughters*; Margaret Blessington, *The Two Friends*; Catherine Gore, *Mrs Armytage, or Female Domination*; Margaret Blessington, *The Victims of Society*; Catherine Gore, *Preferment, or My Uncle the Earl*

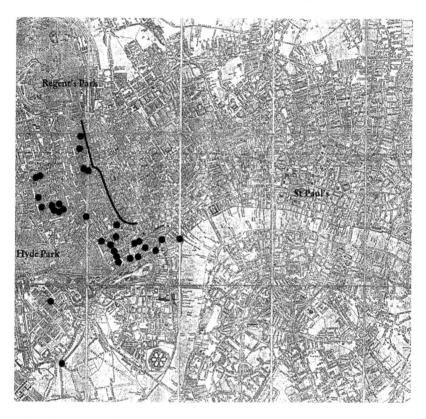

●   residences of main characters

──   Regent Street

A city is uniform only in appearance. Even its name takes on a different sound in the different neighbourhoods. In no other place – with the exception of dreams – can the phenomenon of the border be experienced in such a pristine form as in cities.

WALTER BENJAMIN, *Passagenwerk*

37. Edward Bulwer-Lytton, *Pelham*

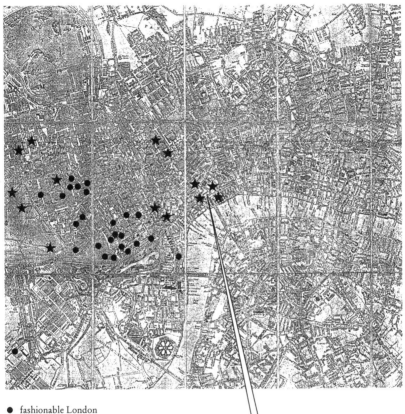

● fashionable London

★ upstarts, mixed society, dangerous classes

We now had entered a part of the town, which was
singularly strange to me; the houses were old, and for
the most part of the meanest description; we appeared
to me to be threading a labyrinth of alleys [. . .] Here
and there, a single lamp shed a sickly light upon the
dismal and intersecting lanes (though lane is too lofty
a word) . . .

EDWARD BULWER-LYTTON, *Pelham*, III.18

38. Jane Austen's London

As the map shows, Austen's London base (her brother's house, in Henrietta Street) is halfway between Darcy and the Gardiners.

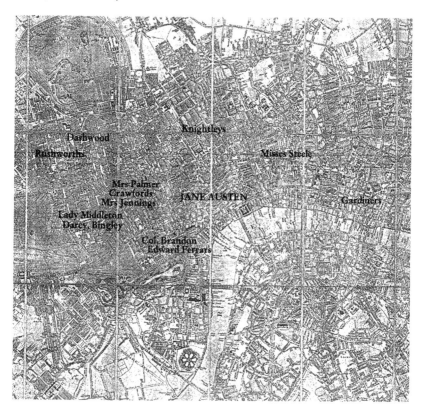

'I think I have heard you say, that their uncle is an attorney in Meryton.'

'Yes; and they have another [Mr Gardiner], who lives somewhere near Cheapside.'

'That is capital,' added her sister, and they both laughed heartily.

'If they had uncles enough to fill all Cheapside,' cried Bingley, 'it would not make them one jot less agreeable.'

'But it must very materially lessen their chance of marrying men of any consideration in the world,' replied Darcy.

To this speech Bingley made no answer . . .

JANE AUSTEN, *Pride and Prejudice*, 8

Hyde Park). And finally, most important of all, the border: Regent Street, the splendid neoclassical barrier erected between 1817 and 1823, as if to lend material support to the class topography of this narrative genre.

How do silver-fork novels address urban complexity, then? Simple: they *reduce* it. Instead of Booth's many-colored London, they give us a binary, black-and-white system: west of Regent Street, one city; east of it, a different one. A perfectly ordered, perfectly legible city; Propp's two worlds, almost. But it's an order which arises not really 'out' of the city, but rather *against* it: in order to make London legible, silver-fork novels must amputate it, erecting a (symbolic) wall that cuts it in halves, from Regent's Park down to Piccadilly. And quite a few readers must have said to themselves: the West End, lovely. But the rest of London? What is there, *what kind of stories* are there, east of Regent Street?

According to Roy Porter, 'Beau Brummell was mortified to be discovered one night as far east as the Strand (he had got lost, he explained)'.[4] In *Pelham* (figure 37), that is also more or less as far east as the story goes; or, better, as far east as the novel 'knows' what London is like. Because the first thing that happens, east of Regent Street, is that roads lose their names. In contrast to the meticulous appraisal of the more and less elegant addresses of the West End, entire areas of London are here lumped wholesale in the same anonymity:[5] around Covent Garden, for instance, Pelham finds himself in 'some of the most ill-favored alleys I ever had the happiness of beholding' (*Pelham*, II.13: remember, when Jane Austen was in

---

[4] Roy Porter, *London. A Social History*, Harvard University Press, Cambridge Mass. 1995, p. 99.
[5] On this point, novel-writing and map-making are perfectly in step with each other. In early nineteenth-century maps, detail is rapidly lost as the map moves away from the West End; the London maps published by Bowles (1823), Wyld (1825), and Fraser (1830), for instance, all agree on the number of streets that intersect Bond Street, or lead into Grosvenor Square – but they are in total disagreement on those that lead into Smithfield (13, 9, 10), or on the alleys around Saffron Hill (in Bowles, one third fewer than in the others), or on the number of lanes that run into the river between Blackfriars and Southwark Bridge (9, 12, 16).

London she lived precisely a few blocks from Covent Garden). And near the end of the book:

> Though all pursuit had long ceased, I still continued to run mechanically, till faint and breathless, I was forced into pausing. I looked round, but could recognize nothing familiar in the narrow and filthy streets; even the names of them were to me like an unknown language.
>
> *Pelham*, III.20

An unknown language. The border has been crossed, and language has immediately sensed it. The geometry of Mayfair gives way to 'a labyrinth of alleys', and Pelham feels so lost[6] he does something no self-respecting dandy should ever do: he runs.[7] It's a minor detail, but it supports the conclusions of the previous chapter: different spaces are not just different landscapes (although they are *also* that, as *Pelham*'s descriptions make perfectly clear): they are different *narrative matrixes*. Each space determines its own kind of actions, its plot – its genre. West of Regent Street, silver-fork novels; and east of it, in the City . . .

In the city, not really City novels, but *Newgate* ones. Stories of crime, of criminals, like *Oliver Twist*; where the metaphor of the labyrinth (that defines *Pelham*'s underworld chapters) returns time and again whenever the story approaches the dangerous classes of Fagin and company. It makes sense, then, for the map of *Oliver Twist* to be the mirror image of *Pelham*: with plenty of sites (and events) to the east of the Temple, and only a couple in the north and the west (the forces of good: Mr Brownlow, the Maylies: figure 39).

A half-London in the silver-fork school; the other half here. But the two halves don't add up to a whole. They may touch briefly and

---

[6] 'To become completely lost is perhaps a rather rare experience for most people in the modern city [. . .] but let the mishap of disorientation once occur, and the sense of anxiety and even terror that accompanies it reveals to us how closely it is linked to our sense of balance and well-being. The very word "lost" in our language means much more than simple geographical uncertainty; it carries overtones of utter disaster' (Lynch, *The Image of the City*, p. 4).

[7] 'Mr Aberton was running up the Rue St. Honoré yesterday . . .'

'*Running!*' cried I, 'just like common people – when were you or I ever seen *running*?' (*Pelham*, I.20).

39. Oliver Twist

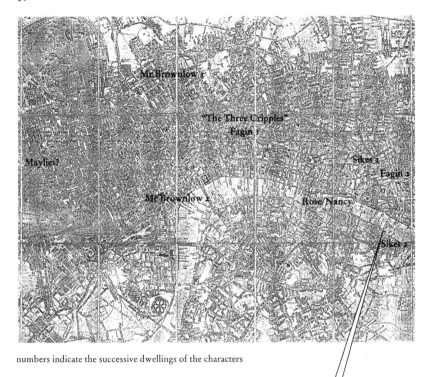

numbers indicate the successive dwellings of the characters

> Near to that part of the Thames on which the church at Rotherhithe abuts, where the buildings on the banks are dirtiest and the vessels on the river blackest with the dust of colliers and the smoke of close-built low-roofed houses, there exists the filthiest, the strangest, the most extraordinary of the many localities that are hidden in London, wholly unknown, even by name, to the great mass of its inhabitants. To reach this place, the visitor has to penetrate through a maze of close, narrow, and muddy streets, thronged by the roughest and poorest of waterside people, and devoted to the traffic they may be supposed to occasion.
>
> CHARLES DICKENS, *Oliver Twist*, 50

in secret, like Rose and Nancy, at midnight, on the no-man's-land of London Bridge: but it's only a moment (that will cost Nancy's life). If a novel focuses on one half of London, it simply cannot *see* the other half, nor represent the crossing of the border between them. When Oliver and Sikes leave for their night expedition, Dickens follows their progress in great detail – until Holborn.[8] Then, the novel skips several miles, and starts again when they are well west of Hyde Park. Strange, considering what Dickens could do with those two in the West End. Instead, there is nothing; and nothing again later, when Nancy seems to fly (and at night, as if to hide the whole scene) from Whitechapel to Hyde Park; or in *Pelham*, where the hero resurfaces directly from the labyrinth of crime into Piccadilly and Whitehall (*Pelham*, II.14, III.20). Even Austen respects the urban taboo: Darcy and the Gardiners (who live, remember, at opposite ends of town) get acquainted, and like each other, and become friends, even: but in a Derbyshire estate. In London, they never meet.

Two half-Londons, that do not add up to a whole. Until a later, much greater novel, where a long coach ride takes two inexperienced young lawyers from a glittering dinner in the West End deep into the night of the Docks.[9] It is Dickens' great wager: to unify the two halves of the city. And his pathbreaking discovery: once the two halves are joined, the result is *more* than the sum of its parts. London becomes not only a larger city (obviously enough), but a more *complex* one; allowing for richer, more unpredictable interactions. But before coming to this, let's have a look at the other capital of the nineteenth-century novel.

---

[8] 'Turning down Sun Street and Crown Street, and crossing Finsbury Square, Mr Sikes struck, by way of Chiswell Stret, into Barbican: thence into Long Lane, and so into Smithfield...' (*Oliver Twist*, 21).

[9] 'The wheels rolled on, and rolled down by the Monument and by the Tower, and by the Docks; down by Ratcliffe, and by Rotherhithe; down by where the accumulated scum of humanity seemed to be washed from higher grounds, like so much moral sewage, and to be pausing until its own weight forced it over the bank and sunk it into the river [...] the wheels rolled on, until they stopped at a dark corner, river-washed and otherwise not washed at all, where the boy alighted and opened the door. [...] "This is a confoundedly out-of-the-way place," said Mortimer, slipping over the stones . . .' (*Our Mutual Friend*, 3).

3. 'A mosaic of little worlds'

Paris. Balzac's Paris, first of all. Figure 40 reproduces the 'demographic plan' of the *Comédie Humaine* elaborated in the 1930s by Norah Stevenson, while figure 41 shows the spaces activated in *Lost Illusions*, the second novel of the Vautrin trilogy. Following Lucien de Rubempré, the novel begins in the Parisian West End (from which Lucien is promptly ejected), and proceeds to a second space, which constitutes its genuine beginning: the world of the Cenacle, of young intellectuals, in the Latin Quarter. Then follows the world of publishing, around the Cité and the Palais Royal; the Theater, further away, on the Boulevards; and finally, the fluid space of journalism, disseminated a bit everywhere: and rightly so, because journalism here embodies *mobility* – spatial, mental, social mobility. Under its sign, Lucien tries in fact to complete his circular movement, and re-enter the closed enclave of the Aristocracy; but he fails, and his trajectory stops at the Frascati, the gambling house that stood, emblematically, on the border between the two social spaces.

How different from the half-cities of the British novel. In *Lost Illusions*, Paris has five, six major spaces, whose borders are crossed and recrossed in the full light of day. It is Robert Park's plural city: a true mosaic of worlds, where the social division of labor seems to have literally stamped itself upon the urban surface: trade near Les Halles, entertainment on the Boulevards, publishing around the Cité, education at the Sorbonne... But the movement between these worlds, on the other hand, is probably less 'quick and easy' than Park had in mind. Richard Sennett:

> The writers of the Chicago school of urban studies believed that movement from neighbourhood to neighbourhood, from scene to scene, was the essence of the 'urban' experience. [. . .] That experience, however, did not belong to all urbanites of the last century equally; it had a class character. As the structure of the quartier and neighbourhood homogenized along economic lines, the people most likely to move from scene to scene were those with interests or connections complicated enough to take them to different parts of the city; such people were the most affluent. Routines of daily life

40. Demography of Balzac's Paris according to Norah Stevenson

Stevenson's work includes a map of the *Comédie*'s main locations, where the most crowded area (shops, theaters, restaurants, cafés) is the triangle formed by rue des Petits Champs, boulevard des Capucines–boulevard des Italiens, and rue Montmartre. Less crowded concentrations are to be found in the Faubourg Saint-Germain (old aristocracy), the Chaussée d'Antin (high finance), Les Halles and the Temple (trade), and the Sorbonne (students). The workers' quarters on the east, both north and south of the Seine, appear quite empty.

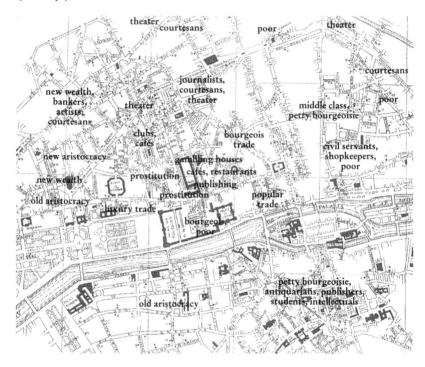

Balzac has established the mythical nature of his world thanks to its specific topographical shape. The landscape of his mythology is Paris. Paris, with its two or three great bankers (Nucingen, du Tillet), Paris, with the great physician Horace Bianchon, the entrepreneur César Birotteau, its four or five cocottes, the usurer Gobseck, the small groups of lawyers and soldiers. But the decisive point is that these figures show up always in the same streets, in the same corners. This means that topography delineates the features of this, as well as of any other mythical space of tradition – and that it may even become its key.

WALTER BENJAMIN, *Passagenwerk*

41. *Lost Illusions*

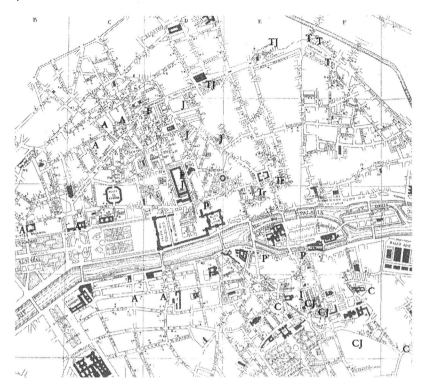

location of social groups

A   aristocracy: chapter 1
C   Cenacle, students: chapters 2,
    4–6, 8–9, 20
F   Frascati gambling house
J   journalism: chapters 7, 17,
    21–30
P   publishing: chapters 3, 10–13
T   theater: chapters 14–16, 18–19
Tr trade

The processes of segregation establish moral distances which make the city a mosaic of little worlds which touch but do not interpenetrate. This makes it possible for individuals to pass quickly and easily from one moral milieu to another, and encourages the fascinating but dangerous experiment of living at the same time in several different contiguous, but otherwise widely separated, worlds. All this tends to give to city life a superficial and adventitious character; it tends to complicate social relationships and to produce new and divergent individual types. It introduces, at the same time, an element of chance and adventure which adds to the stimulus of city life and gives it, for young and fresh nerves, a peculiar attractiveness.

ROBERT E. PARK, 'The City: Suggestions for the Investigation of Human Behaviour in the Urban Environment' passed outside the quartier were becoming bourgeois urban experience; the sense of being cosmopolitan and membership in the bourgeois classes thus came to have an affinity. Conversely, localism and lower class fused.[10]

A city where movement cannot be taken for granted: Zola's novels will be its most powerful – inexorable – image. It is the naturalist *milieu* of figure 42: the space that catches human beings by their throat, and doesn't let go; the murderous space of Döblin's Alexanderplatz. And this is already partially true for *Lost Illusions*, where Lucien's initial experience is less one of movement, than of *frustrated* movement: expelled from the Faubourg Saint-Honoré, slighted by publishers and journalists, ridiculed at the Opéra and the Champs Elysées . . . And as for the Latin Quarter, it is a torment for this sensual and ambitious young man, whom the Conciergerie will remind precisely 'of his first room in Paris, in the rue de Cluny': cold garrets, bad food, old clothes, no women, no money . . .

[10] Richard Sennett, *The Fall of Public Man*, Knopf, New York 1977, pp. 136–7.

---

42. Zola's Paris

Zola's Paris novels are mostly confined to very small spaces, whose boundaries are crossed only on special occasions (the wedding in *L'Assommoir*, Lisa's expedition to the Palais de Justice in *The Belly of Paris*), or else, at the risk of one's life (Nana's agony at the Grand-Hôtel; the slaughter on the Boulevard Montmartre, in *The Belly of Paris*; Coupeau, in *L'Assommoir*, who is fished out of the Seine at the Pont-Neuf, and dies at the Sainte-Anne Hospital, near Montparnasse). Significantly, the novel with the most 'open' pattern is *Nana*, which does not represent a homogeneous social space, but the uneasy interaction between high society, theater, and prostitution. (The house owned by Nana at the apex of her fortune, in the rue Villiers, lies however outside the map, at some distance from the high bourgeois area of the Chaussée d'Antin). Incidentally, Nana is also responsible for the main spatial transgressions of *L'Assommoir*, around the rue du Caire and the outer boulevards.

The lack of urban mobility has its counterpart in the frequent long-distance movements of human beings as well as things. The claustrophobic department store of *The Ladies' Paradise*, for instance, owes its triumph to commodities imported from a dozen European and Asian countries; while the 'Banque Universelle', in *L'Argent*, speculates on the Mediterranean and the Middle East. The international theme is widespread in *Nana* (who herself travels to Egypt and Russia), and takes a sinister turn in *The Belly of Paris*, with Florent's exile to Cayenne.

A *L'Assommoir*	★ *L'Argent*	● *The Ladies' Paradise*
N *Nana*	□ *The Belly of Paris*	—— The day of the wedding (*L'Assommoir*)

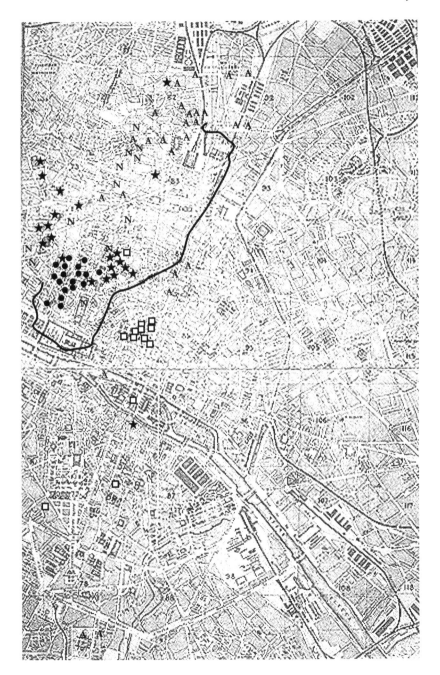

But after a couple of fortunate articles, Lucien's Paris suddenly changes. On the short happy day of figure 43, he still wakes up in the Latin Quarter, but leaves it early in the morning and never returns. In a few hours, he visits all the spaces that had previously rejected him, impressing them with his recent success. 'Living at the same time in contiguous, but otherwise widely separate worlds' had been Park's

---

43. Lucien de Rubempré: the day of success (chapters 21–25)

Lucien's day begins at his student flat in the rue de Cluny (1), from where he goes to Lousteau's (2), and then to Florine's (3). From there, he and Lousteau go to Félicien Vernou's (4), and then to Coralie's flat (5). Here begins the more public part of Lucien's day; he goes with Coralie to the editorial offices (6), then to the Bois de Boulogne (7: not included in the map), and finally to Véry's restaurant (8), in the Palais Royal. Leaving Coralie, Lucien talks to authors and publishers in the Wooden Galleries, also located in the Palais Royal (9), then meets Lousteau again, returns with him to the newspaper (10), and ends his day at the Boulevard theaters (11, 12). With the exception of his early morning walk, Lucien is never alone during this very long day. Think of Raskolnikov, with his interminable solitary rambles through Petersburg.

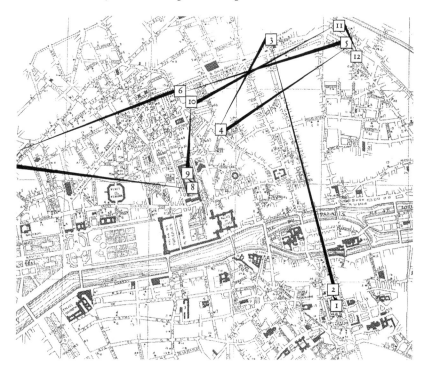

definition of urban experience; 'fascinating, but dangerous experiment', he had added. Fascinating, yes, in the day of triumph. But also dangerous, in the 'fateful week' that follows it as a sort of perverse repetition, when the cooperation of several independent agents – the complexity of the urban system – plays *against* the individual, rather than for him. In figure 44, for instance, the bankers of the Chaussée

44. The fateful week

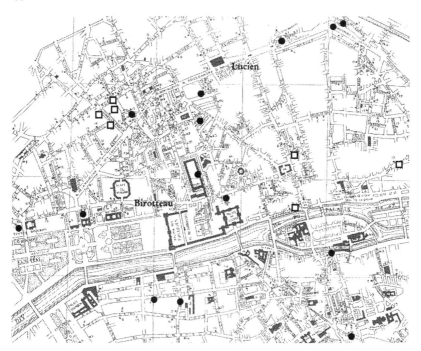

● Lucien's antagonists

☐ Birotteau's antagonists

In the lives of ambitious people and all those whose success depends on the aid they get from men and things [. . .] a cruel moment comes when some power or other subjects them to severe trials. Everything goes wrong at once, from every side threads break or become entangled and misfortune looms at every point of the compass. When a man loses his head among this moral chaos, he is lost [. . .] So then, to every man who is not born rich comes what we must call his fateful week. For Napoleon it was the week of the retreat from Moscow.

This cruel moment had come for Lucien . . .

HONORÉ DE BALZAC, *Lost Illusions*, II.38

d'Antin, who refuse César Birotteau the loan that would save him, have no connection with his landlord lurking 'like a spider' in the Cour Batave, or with the hazelnut wholesaler of rue Perret-Gasselin that causes Birotteau's first troubles, or the upholsterer of the Faubourg Saint-Antoine; as a matter of fact, they ignore each other's

---

45. Parvenir! The drive from the provinces to Paris in nineteenth-century novels

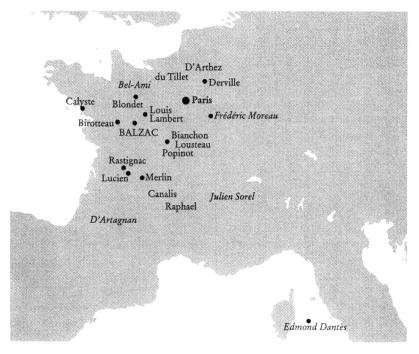

plain type: characters from the *Comédie Humaine*
italics: characters from other novels

Paris is a meeting place, swarming with talent, for all the forceful vigorous young men who spring up like wild seedlings in French soil. They haven't a roof over their heads, but they are equal to anything, and set on making their fortune. Your humble servant was just such a young man in his time, and I have known some others!

HONORÉ DE BALZAC, *Cousin Bette*

existence. And yet, in a sinister parody of Smith's invisible hand, all these 'contiguous, but otherwise widely separate worlds' join forces – without trying to, and indeed *without even knowing it* – in hunting down and then murdering Birotteau (or Coralie in *Lost Illusions*). It is Balzac's marketplace: independent agents, egoistical aims, rational calculations – and corpses.

A step backwards, and a few more words on the Latin Quarter. A precocious product of the urban division of labor, this space of high learning, established in the late middle ages and unchanged ever since, is also, and in Balzac first of all, *the world of youth*: converging from all over France towards this square mile 'set on making their fortune' (figure 45). Or better, they arrive – and then immediately want to move on. Look at figures 46*ab*: at the beginning, Balzac's young men are indeed all there, in a handful of streets around the Sorbonne. But they quickly realize that their objects of desire – in Balzac's world, a very simple notion: women, and money – are all elsewhere: in the Faubourg Saint-Germain and Saint-Honoré, in the Chaussée d'Antin, in the *demi-monde* of the Boulevards. Far away. It's the basic matrix of Balzac's narrative: two poles, and a current that discharges itself – *parvenir!* – from one to the other. And the magnetism of desire 'orients' the city along the axis described years ago by Pierre Bourdieu: from the *rive gauche*, towards the 'beehive' in the north-west. The desire of youth makes Paris *legible*, selecting from the city's complicated system a clear point of departure, and one of arrival.

And in the long interim, between the two extremes of Paris another typically urban experience takes shape: daydreams. Grand projects, erotic fantasies, imaginary revenges, sudden epiphanies... And all this, always in the same space, exactly *midway between the world of youth and that of desire* (figure 46*c*). It is the public space of the Tuileries and the Champs Elysées, with its oblique gazes and ephemeral meetings; more icastically still, the no-man's-land of the bridges suspended across the Seine. It is in a store on the Quai that Raphaël de Valentin finds the talisman of Balzac's fairy-tale ('Desire, and your desires shall be realized': *The Wild Ass's Skin*); it is on the

46a. Arrival in Paris

The map includes several novels of the *Comédie Humaine* and a couple of characters from *Sentimental Education* (Lucien 1 refers to *Lost Illusions*, and Lucien 2 to *A Harlot High and Low*). In a stroke of genius, Balzac's most ambitious young man – Rastignac – is initially placed in 'the grimmest part of Paris', at the opposite pole from the world of social success.

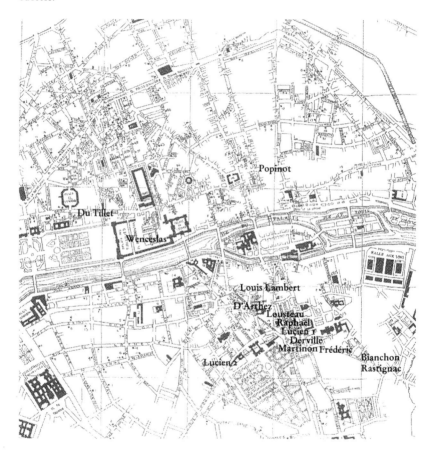

During the first days of his stay at the Hôtel de Cluny, Lucien, like any newcomer, was shy and conventional in his behaviour. [. . .] He plunged into his work with that initial ardour soon dissipated by the difficulties and diversions which Paris offers to every kind of existence, the most luxurious and the most denuded. To get the better of them, the savage energy of real talent or the grim willpower of ambition is needed.

HONORÉ DE BALZAC, *Lost Illusions*, II.2

46b. 'That splendid world he had wished to conquer'

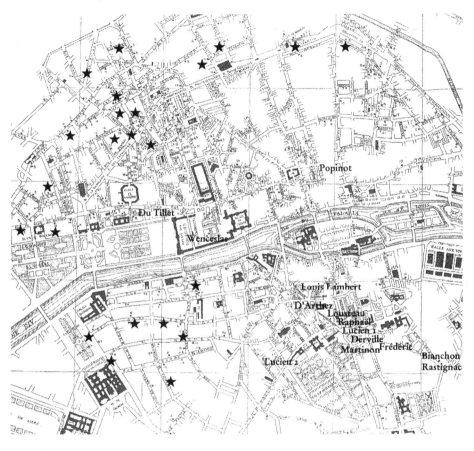

★ objects of desire

Left alone, Rastignac walked a few steps to the highest part of the cemetery, and saw Paris spread out below on both banks of the winding Seine. Lights were beginning to twinkle here and there. His gaze fixed almost avidly upon the space that lay between the column of the Place Vendôme and the dome of the Invalides; there lay the splendid world that he had wished to conquer. He eyed that humming hive with a look that foretold its despoliation, as if he already felt on his lips the sweetness of its honey, and said with superb defiance: 'it's war, between us two!'

And as the first act of his challenge to society, Rastignac went to dine with Madame de Nucingen.

HONORÉ DE BALZAC, *Old Goriot*

46c. Daydreams

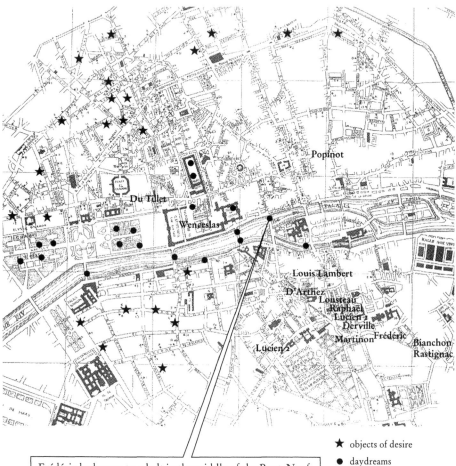

★ objects of desire
● daydreams

Frédéric had come to a halt in the middle of the Pont-Neuf;
baring his chest and hatless, he filled his lungs with air. He
could feel a surge of inexhaustible power rising from the
depths of his being, a flood of tenderness which set his nerves
vibrating like the lapping waves before his eyes. A church
clock struck slowly, like a voice calling to him.

Thrills ran through his body; he felt he was being lifted
into a higher world. He had been vouchsafed some extraordinary faculty of whose purpose he had no idea. He wondered,
seriously, whether to become a great poet or a great painter . . .

GUSTAVE FLAUBERT, *Sentimental Education*, I.4

46d. The end

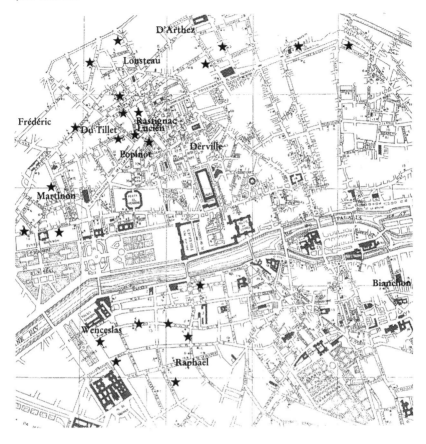

The hero-agent is the one who crosses the border of the plot-field [. . .] once he has crossed the border, he enters another semantic field, an 'anti-field' vis-à-vis the initial one. If movement is to cease, he has to merge with the field, and be transformed from a mobile into an immobile persona. If this does not happen, the plot sequence is not concluded and movement continues.

JURII M. LOTMAN, *The Structure of the Artistic Text*

Quai that Lucien and Frédéric find new quarters, in their march towards the great world; it is from his balcony on the Seine, 'gazing down at the river', that the latter spends day after day, looking 'through' Paris towards the home of his impossible love:

> When he had finished looking at the stone bridge of Notre-Dame [. . .] he'd always turn away to gaze in the direction of the quai aux Ormes [. . .] Rising above a jumble of roofs in front of him were the Tour-Saint-Jacques, the Hotel de Ville and the churches of Saint-Gervais, Saint-Louis and Saint-Paul; to the east, the Spirit of Liberty on top of the Bastille column shone like a large gold star, while to the west the massive blue dome of the Tuileries Palace stood out against the sky. Somewhere behind there, in the same direction, must be Madame Arnoux's house.
>
> *Sentimental Education*, I.5

A Paris oriented by desire, and held together by *reverie* (until the hero 'arrives', and the tension falls: figure 46*d*). Specific stories are the product of specific spaces, I have often repeated; and now, the corollary of that thesis: *without a certain kind of space, a certain kind of story is simply impossible.* Without the Latin Quarter, I mean, and its tension with the rest of Paris, we wouldn't have the wonder of the French *Bildungsroman*, nor that image of youth – hungry, dreamy, ambitious – that has been its greatest invention. Think of the rival traditions, in Germany, Britain, Russia: all great literatures, without question; but they all lack a symbolic equivalent of the *rive gauche* – and so, they fall short of the intensity of Paris. Think of Pip's London, or David Copperfield's, or Pendennis': all of them caught in the gray universe of Inns of Court, so that the city can never become an object of desire.[11] He who does not know the left bank of the Seine between the rue Saint-Jacques and the rue des Saints-Pères doesn't

---

[11] When Lucien arrives in Paris, he immediately goes to the Boulevards and the Tuileries, where he discovers 'the luxury of the shops, the height of the buildings, the busy to-and-fro of carriages, the ever-present contrast between extreme luxury and extreme indigence [. . .] young people with their happy, care-free air [. . .] divinely dressed and divinely beautiful women'. When Pip arrives in London, his first walk takes him to Smithfield ('the shameful place, being all asmear with filth and fat and blood and foam'), Saint Paul's, and Newgate, where he sees a crowd of drunkards, the gallows, the whipping post, and 'the Debtors' Door, out of which culprits came to be hanged'. No wonder Pip falls mortally ill.

know life, says Balzac in *Old Goriot*, and he is right. How much did British culture lose, by not having a Latin Quarter?

4. *Fear in Paris*

Balzac's city; and then Sue's, with that fantastic title, *The Mysteries of Paris*. And yet, tracing the novel's geography, one is struck by how hollow Sue's Paris is – depopulated, almost: no Latin Quarter, no trade, no theater, no *demi-monde*, no finance . . . (figure 47). The two great antagonists – Prince Rudolphe of Gerolstein, and Countess Sarah MacGregor – are not even French: they converge on Paris, like James Bond and the Spectre, to play their dangerous game, but they could be in London, or Madrid, and nothing would change; they even live a little out of the way (the ruthless Sarah, in the same street where Balzac had lived for ten years . . .) Marx is right, this is not a social conflict, but a moral crusade replicating itself at every new engagement: in Rudolphe's patrician mansion near the Champs Elysées or in the popular dwellings of the Faubourg Saint-Antoine; in the bourgeois lair of rue Sentier, or in the underworld of the Cité.

Against the background of this *paysage moralisé*, Sue's other great novelty stands out: the overlap of the urban plot with the 'family romance' of Fleur-de-Marie. For her true identity to be finally revealed, the novel must run a thread through the Cité (at the center of Paris: where Rudolphe 'saves' the girl in the novel's opening scene), rue Cassini (to the south; where the Chouette reveals her identity to Sarah MacGregor, who is the girl's mother), rue du Temple (to the east; where Madame Pipelet reveals to Rudolphe Fleur-de-Marie's presence in the Saint-Lazare prison, which lies for its part beyond the Boulevards), rue Sentier (to the north: the study of the notary Ferrand, who sold her as a child, before the novel's beginning), and rue Plumet (to the south-west, in the Faubourg Saint-Germain: the house of the father, where the agnition between Rudolphe and Fleur-de-Marie can finally occur). The city turns into a large puzzle, whose separate spaces acquire meaning in the light of

47. The mysteries of Paris

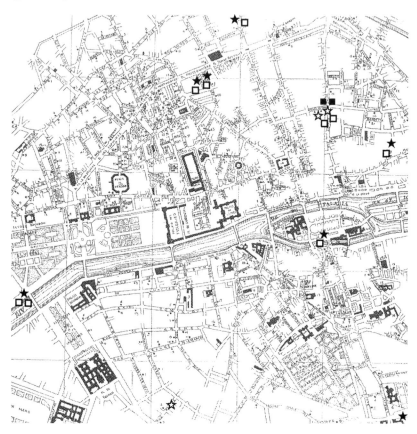

☆ forces of good

★ forces of evil

□ offensives of the forces of good

■ offensives of the forces of evil

'Angels shall come forth and separate the good from the evil ones' (Matthew, XIII, 49) [. . .] Rudolphe transforms himself into one of these angels. He traverses the world to separate the good from the evil ones, in order to punish the latter, and reward the former. The representation of good and evil has stamped itself so deeply in his feeble brain that he believes in the physical existence of Satan, and would like to catch him alive, as the famous prof. Sack of Bonn. On the other hand, he tries to reproduce on a small scale the devil's antithesis, God. He loves to 'jouer un peu le rôle de la providence'. Just as, in reality, all distinctions converge more and more into the distinction of poor and rich, so in the idea all aristocratic distinctions end up in the opposition of good and evil. This distinction is the last form given by the aristocrat to his prejudices.

KARL MARX, *The Holy Family*

an individual destiny: a 'humanization' of the metropolis that returns in Dickens' late novels, and that I will later examine at length.

In the meantime, another mystery of Paris: the urban legend *ante litteram* of the Court of Miracles, which makes its first appearance (as Roger Chartier has shown) in a map of Paris of 1652 – at the very moment, that is, when the Great Internment of the beggars and homeless of Paris has in fact just *suppressed* it.[12] And yet, this space that no longer exists returns in map after map, for almost two centuries. Why? And later still, when its memory must have been even paler, it becomes Hugo's great urban myth. Again: why?

A step backwards. The Court of Miracles, explains Chartier, is not a unique phenomenon, but the hyperbolic image of a reality – the *cul-de-sac* – that is ubiquitous in Paris, where it offers a shelter to those 'demeurant partout' (the homeless, as we would call them) who are suspected of all sorts of crimes. Figure 48, based on Robert de Vaugondy's *Plan de la Ville et des Faubourgs de Paris* (1771), gives an idea of the situation; while figure 49 reproduces the section of Vaugondy's original where the *Cour des Miracles* is located. Now, it is striking how many *culs-de-sac* there are, especially along the north–south commercial axis, and near the Seine; how widespread are these urban 'cysts', as Chartier calls them. If they were really spaces of illegalism, the threat must have been endemic indeed.

Whence, possibly, the reason for the Court's obstinate presence: by enclosing illegality within a limited (and slightly peripheral) space, it makes it easier to recognize. Chartier's oxymoron – 'a concentration of marginals' – is perfect: the Court of Miracles is such a powerful myth because it groups together what is confused, unpredictable, random. By circumscribing the *Lumpenproletariat* of early modern times in its neat little rectangle, the Court is itself a (symbolic) version of the Great Internment: the Great Classification, as it

---

[12] 'Around the middle of the seventeenth century, the time of the great concentrations [of marginals] is over': Roger Chartier, *La "monarchie d'argot" entre le mythe et l'histoire*, in *Les Marginaux et les exclus dans l'histoire*, Union Générale d'Editions, Paris 1979 (I quote from the Italian translation, *Figure della furfanteria*, Istituto della Enciclopedia Italiana, Roma 1984: especially pp. 39 ff.).

48. Parisian cul-de-sacs according to Robert de Vaugondy (1771)

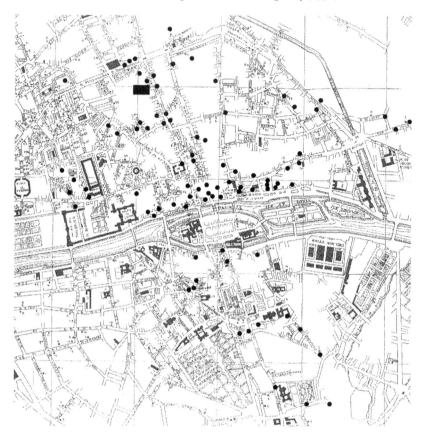

● cul-de-sac
▮ Court of Miracles

The Court of Miracles, located in the rue neuve-Saint-Sauveur, is not separated from the other gathering places of the dangerous poor (unrepentant beggars and potential criminals) present within the urban space. From the late sixteenth to the mid seventeenth century, these gathering places are basically of two kinds: the city's peripheries, and the blind alleys [∴.] The small courts and blind alleys that offer repair to the *demeurants partout* are extremely abundant in the topography of modern Paris: in the preface to his 1701 map, Jean de la Caille mentions 74 cul-de-sacs; Delharme, in 1763, 90; Vaugondy, in 1776, 108; Verniquet, in 1791, 104. The very texture of Parisian space is an invitation to form these small or large 'cysts', populated by those who cannot count on any form of property.

ROGER CHARTIER, 'La "monarchie d'argot" entre le mythe et l'histoire' were. And with this, we have reached the conceptual focus of the present chapter.

5. Theoretical interlude III. Stories of the Third

Cities can be very random environments, I said of Booth's map at the beginning of this chapter, and novels protect their readers from randomness by reducing it. The half-London of the silver-fork and of the Newgate novels; the struggle between Good and Evil in *The Mysteries of Paris*; Hugo's 'concentration of marginals': here are

49. A section of Robert de Vaugondy's 1771 *Plan de la Ville et des Faubourgs de Paris*

some of the many *simplifications* of the urban system, that make it easier to grasp, and to inhabit.

But Balzac is different. Instead of protecting the novel from the complications of Paris, he sees them as a fantastic *opportunity* for narrative structure: for the novel of complexity, as I have called it. But what does this mean?

Let me begin with the how, the morphological side of the question. The first novelty of Balzac's Paris – and it leaps to the eye, if one thinks of Sue, or Hugo – is the social diversity of its plot: old aristocracy, new financial wealth, middle-class trade, *demi-monde*, professionals, servants, young intellectuals, clerks, criminals . . . All these social groups – second novelty – interact all the time, in many directions, and in ever new combinations. And, basically, this is it. Independent agents, and composite interactions: here is the (simple) matrix which produces the (complex) city of the *Comédie Humaine*: the *roulette*-city of figure 33, where minor actions are easily magnified (in a sort of 'butterfly effect') into major results. In *Cousin Pons*, a Marais concierge wants to steal a few hundred francs from a dying tenant – and her swindle generates several hundred thousand for a usurer of the rue Royale (one mile to the west), and a few millions for a Count of the Chaussée d'Antin (another mile to the west). In *Old Goriot*, Rastignac mentions the name of Madame de Beauséant (which means: Faubourg Saint-Germain), and the doors of Paris' great world fly open before him; then he mentions Goriot (which means: 'the grimmest quarter of Paris'), and those doors are barred. A moment, a careless word, can change everything.

Many subjects interacting in more than one way: and a new epoch begins for the European novel. And usually, with new epochs, we insist precisely on the new: on how unlikely the formal shift was, and how striking its realization. But here, to be honest, the real question is the opposite one. Since Balzac's basic ingredients are so few, and so simple, *why had no one ever figured them out*? What made such a simple step so difficult to take?

Figure 34, at the end of the previous chapter, showed how the founding work of modern narrative theory – Vladimir Propp's *Morphology of the Folktale* – rests on the existence of two antithetical spaces from whose opposition arise all the fundamental events of the plot. Now, in the course of the twentieth century, Propp's model has been complicated and criticized in several ways, but this binary foundation has never been really challenged. Lévi-Strauss' mythical matrixes, Lotman's fields, Greimas' semiotic square: despite their differences, all these models agree with the *Morphology* on the decisive point: the precondition of narrative is a binary opposition.[13] Two fields. And, let it be clear, there are excellent reasons for this. A story is a system of actions, and an action requires (at least) two actors, with their relative spaces: an oppositional pair is thus necessary – and very often sufficient. No wonder, then, that narratology has adopted a binary model: it captures the basic, fundamental requirement that no story can ever do without.

This narratological argument overlaps with the socio-historical one recalled at the beginning of this section. Cities can be very random environments, I said, and novels try as a rule to reduce such randomness; this reduction, we can now add, typically *takes the form of a binary system*: the unpredictable urban elements are all pigeon-holed, all classified in two well-defined fields: the half-Londons, the 'concentration of marginals', the clashing armies of Rudolphe and of Sarah. Most urban novels *simplify* the urban system by turning it into a neat oppositional pattern which is much easier to read.

And it makes perfect sense, an over-complicated environment requires a symbolic form capable of mastering it. It makes sense – except for Balzac. Who revels in the complications of Paris, as the *poli*-centric map of *Lost Illusions* made immediately clear. But why on earth did he do it – why replace a binary structure with a plurality of agents? Binary stories had existed since the beginning of time, and they were often quite good. The pattern had been weakened and

---

[13] All these thinkers, incidentally, conceptualize narrative in markedly *spatial* terms – most clearly Greimas, the 'profound spatiality of [whose] system' is discussed by Fredric Jameson in his intelligent Foreword to *On Meaning*, Minnesota University Press, 1987, pp. xv, xxi–xxii.

'deformed' by the advent of the novel, true (I pointed it out in the first chapter); but had not been superseded by a different one. Until Balzac. And one wonders, again: how did he do it? And why?

A plurality of agents. Better: *three* agents. This is the Open Sesame of Balzac's narrative: a deep structure which is *just as clearly delimited* as the binary one – but different. Triangular. The field of the hero, of the antagonist, and then a *third* narrative pole; and a plot that in the course of time becomes more and more the story of this third pole. The story of the Third. Of an independent, autonomous Third.[14]

But who is this Third, and what stories does it produce? In Balzac (and in Dickens), the answer is always the same: the Third is *the figure of social overdetermination*, which intersects the narrative line, and changes its course. The concrete embodiment of this third force changes from novel to novel, of course: it can be the aristocratic Madame de Beauséant of *Old Goriot*, who shifts Rastignac's desire from Anastasie to Delphine, or the great criminal Vautrin, who almost shifts it again, towards Victorine; in *Lost Illusions*, it's the nervous world of journalism, halfway between the two great Balzacian fields of the Latin Quarter and the Faubourg Saint-Germain. The Third can be Paris itself ('between Madame de Bargeton and Lucien a mutual disenchantment was taking place, whose cause was Paris': *Lost Illusions*); or money, which always intervenes between Balzac's young men and their desires. But if the content of the Third changes, its function is constant; Georg Simmel describes it as 'transition, conciliation, and the abandonment of absolute contrast'.[15] And thus Julien Freund, who develops Simmel's insight into a 'polémologie', or science of conflict:

[14] Independent, hence different from Propp's 'donor', Girard's 'mediator', or Pavel's 'auxiliary', which are all functionally *subordinated* to the protagonist, and as a consequence don't modify the binary nature of the narrative.

[15] Georg Simmel, *Soziologie*, 1908, in Kurt H. Wolff, ed., *The Sociology of Georg Simmel*, The Free Press, New York 1964, p. 145.

The third can accomplish a twofold task. On the one hand, it can prevent the onset of war, in so far as it hinders the formation of a bipolar relation [...] On the other, the Third may appear in the course of a conflict, and modify its bilateral relation of forces [...] in general, its intervention leads to the conclusion of the conflict, usually by way of a compromise.[16]

Compromise, this is the key. The Third enters these novels as the force of social mediation; and then – decisive passage – mediation itself *becomes the true protagonist of the Comédie Humaine*. It's such a strange idea for narrative morphology, this replacement of conflict with mediation, such a paradigm shift, that it takes time for the pattern to crystallize. In 1831, in the first great Paris novel, *The Wild Ass's Skin*, the autonomous Third does not yet exist, and its place is still occupied by Propp's magic object; in 1834, in *Old Goriot*, the Third makes its appearance in some great lonely characters (Madame de Beauséant, Vautrin, Goriot himself: significantly, all *defeated* as the story unfolds); in 1839, in the Parisian section of *Lost Illusions*, the Third acquires the ubiquitous form of entire social groups (publishing, theater, journalism) and becomes invincible. And at this point the narrative hierarchy reverses itself: the melodramatic polarization of the earlier novels – 'the logic of the excluded middle', in Peter Brooks' elegant formula for melodrama – recedes, while 'the middle' of universal mediation, far from being excluded, occupies the foreground.

I have presented a narratological account of the rise of the Third – but I hope it is clear that this rather abstract geometry is in its turn a profoundly *historical* product: it is really the secret shape of the city, where the indirect – triangular – nature of social relations becomes unmistakable and unavoidable. In the end, this is what 'forces' Balzac to modify Propp's binary structure: he is trying to write the story of the city-as-market – where A sells to B in order to buy from C, and C sells to A in order to buy from D, or E, and so on, in the endless chain of what Marx called the 'three *dramatis personae*' of the exchange process. And in order to capture this underlying structure of the city,

---

[16] Julien Freund, 'Le rôle du tiers dans les conflits', *Études polémologiques*, 17, 1975.

a binary narrative configuration is not enough – it's wrong, actually: it misses the point. But not so compromise: it is the sign of the Third; and, after Balzac, the sign of urban existence itself.

As in all markets, then, the heroes of Balzac's urban novels may well make a fortune, but they never find what they really wanted, because in the great game of social triangulation the idea of a meaningful aim becomes weaker, and finally vanishes.[17] 'Your results give the lie to your initial principles', says Jacques Collin to his last disciple (whose life he will buy with a bag of gold): between principles and results, Freund's compromise has found its way. To have found a way to represent compromise – actually, more: *to have turned compromise into a fascinating event*, thanks to a narrative structure of unprecedented complexity – is the greatest achievement, and the greatest misery, of the *Comédie Humaine*.

6. *Fields of power*

So far, the maps in this chapter have placed characters in their specific urban locations. Figures 50 and 51, inspired by Pierre Bourdieu's work on Flaubert, try for their part to visualize their meeting places, and their interactions. In *Lost Illusions*, for instance, the maximum mix is reached at Lucien's and Coralie's party, where four of the novel's six main social groups are present: journalism (on the left side of the diagram), trade (right), the young intellectuals of the Cenacle (bottom), and the theater (center). There is nobody from publishing (Dauriat, Barbet, etc.); and nobody – a far more significant absence – from the aristocratic world of the Faubourg

---

[17] Lucien has an appointment with D'Arthez at Flicoteaux's; but Lousteau shows up, and Lucien moves to his table. Later on, at the Luxembourg, the two mean to talk about poetry – but slide quickly into journalism. Lucien's first encounter with journalism occurs – at the theater. Between the theater and Lucien – Coralie. And so on, one episode after the other: each binary configuration opens up, and gives rise to a triangle. In fact, the Third is present even in the most intimate moments: Rastignac's and Delphine's apartment is paid for – by Goriot (who meanwhile is dying at the opposite end of Paris). And the same between Lucien and Coralie: Camusot pays for their night of passion – and shows up the next morning, while Lucien is still asleep.

Saint-Germain. The latter shows up elsewhere, at the Panorama-Dramatique, or the Ambigu, with the Duke of Rhetoré and the German Diplomat: but when the aristocracy appears, the Cenacle immediately vanishes. Every meeting place, in Balzac, is also a space of exclusion: open to some, and closed to others. A fact that becomes crystal clear at the end of the novel, in the dinners at the Faubourg

---

50. The field of power in *Lost Illusions*

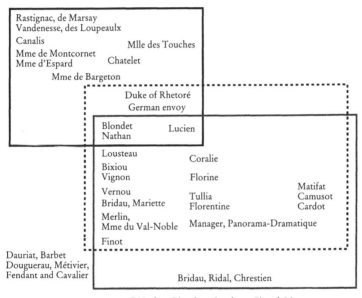

Rastignac, de Marsay
Vandenesse, des Loupeaulx
Canalis   Mlle des Touches
Mme de Montcornet
Mme d'Espard   Chatelet
    Mme de Bargeton

Duke of Rhetoré
German envoy

Blondet   Lucien
Nathan

Lousteau
            Coralie
Bixiou
Vignon   Florine
Vernou   Matifat
Bridau, Mariette   Tullia   Camusot
                    Florentine Cardot
Merlin,
Mme du Val-Noble   Manager, Panorama-Dramatique
Finot

Dauriat, Barbet
Douguerau, Métivier,
Fendant and Cavalier   Bridau, Ridal, Chrestien

D'Arthez, Bianchon, Lambert, Giraud, Meyraux

☐ Faubourg Saint-Germain

⌐⌐⌐⌐ Panorama-Dramatique, Ambigu

☐ Lucien and Coralie

The aristocracy is, in a sense, the mind of society, just as the bourgeoisie and the working class are the organism and its action – whence the need for different forces to inhabit different residences [. . .] Isn't this space that distances a social class [the aristocracy of the Faubourg Saint-Germain] from the entire city the material consecration of the moral divide that must keep them apart?

HONORÉ DE BALZAC, *The Duchess of Langeais*

51. The field of power in *Sentimental Education*

Although Flaubert's hero occupies the center of this figure, the periphery of the diagram is also significant, as it delineates a topography of resentment: Deslauriers (whose feeling of exclusion is if anything sharpened by the ephemeral invitation by Dambreuse, after 1848), the actor Delmar, the 'citizen' Régimbart, and especially Sénécal, who is, with Dussardier, the protagonist of the military showdown of December 1851. In general, political activism is presented in the novel as a (vain) surrogate of economic power.

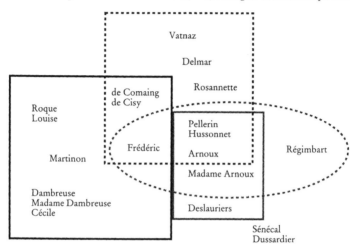

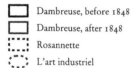

Dambreuse, before 1848
Dambreuse, after 1848
Rosannette
L'art industriel

In *Sentimental Education* Flaubert presents us with a generative model. The first element of this model is a representation of the structure of the ruling class, or, as I put it, of the field of power. The social space described in this work is organized around two poles represented on the one hand by the art dealer Arnoux and on the other by the banker Dambreuse. [. . .] To reconstruct this social space, I simply noted methodically just who attends the different meetings or gatherings or dinners [. . .] The receptions organized by Rosannette, the *demi-mondaine*, bring people from these two worlds together. Her world, the *demi-monde*, is an in-between, intermediate world. [. . .] *Education* may be read as an experimental novel in the true sense of the term. Flaubert first offers us a description of the field of power, within which he traces the movements of six young men, including Frédéric, who are propelled in it like so many particles in a magnetic field. And each one's trajectory – what we normally call the history of his life – is determined by the interaction between the forces of the field and his own inertia.

PIERRE BOURDIEU, *The Rules of Art*

Saint-Germain, where the aristocracy is present *en masse*, but apart from two or three journalists, all others are firmly kept out.

All spaces include some groups, and exclude others; better, they include some groups *because* they exclude the others, and much of Balzac's pathos lies precisely in these invisible class lines; in the pressures and counterpressures to traverse them, or to reject the ambitious intruder. There is no harsher illustration of this than *A Harlot High and Low*, where the five or six spaces of *Lost Illusions* are reduced to two, and where one could easily draw a line that cuts Paris in half: a Regent Street, a meridian of the Tuileries, along which Jacques Collin deploys his troops, trying to 'force open the doors of the Faubourg Saint-Germain' for Lucien (figure 52). But it's all in vain, and his defeat is encapsulated in a detail of the lower part of the map: the Church of Saint-Thomas-d'Aquin, in the middle of the Faubourg Saint-Germain, where Lucien should marry Clotilde de Grandlieu: a wedding that never takes place. And the Church of Saint-Germain-des-Prés, towards the Latin Quarter, where Lucien's funeral takes place, after his suicide in prison. A thousand meters, no more, between these two churches; and *Harlot* is the tragedy of those thousand meters.

Paris as a battlefield . . . *Harlot* is *Lost Illusions'* continuation, of course, but in a deeper sense it is its drastic *simplification*, which returns Balzac's narrative structure from the new policentric model to the old binary matrix: field, and anti-field; Parisian West End, and City of Crime. It is a turnaround, a retreat, that shows how difficult the novel of complexity could be. Difficult, because of the many variables that must be simultaneously followed, and the energy that the task requires; and because the model is so new (and so strange) that even its inventor may well miss its deeper structural logic. No wonder, then, that Balzac yields to simplification, and reverts to that binary paradigm that *Lost Illusions* had so memorably overcome; morphological change occurs often like this, a little blindly, with formal breakthroughs that are indeed *realized*, but not really *recognized*. And indeed, the other storyteller of the nineteenth-century city shows exactly the same oscillation.

52. Vautrin's last battle

Of all the characters that live near the symbolic border of Paris' West End (Esther, Lucien, Peyrade, Lydia), not one survives the conflict between the opposite social worlds. The difficulty of penetrating the world of the élite is confirmed by the four residences of the *demimondaine* Madame Schontz in the novel *Béatrix*: all just a few blocks away from the Chaussée d'Antin – but none of them actually in it. Something similar will later happen in Zola's *Nana*.

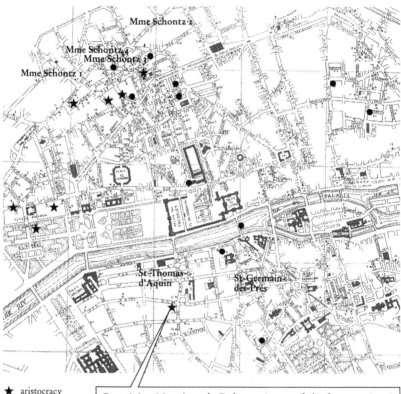

★   aristocracy

●   underworld

Perceiving Monsieur de Rubempré, one of the footmen [. . .] plants himself at the top of the steps and stands before the door like a soldier returning to sentry-duty. 'His Grace is not at home!' said the man. 'Madame la Duchesse can receive me', Lucien pointed out to the footman. 'Madame la Duchesse is out', the man gravely replies. 'Mademoiselle Clotilde . . .' 'I do not think Mademoiselle Clotilde could see Monsieur in the absence of Madame la Duchesse . . .' 'But there are people here', replied Lucien, conscious of the blow. 'I don't know', says the footman.

HONORÉ DE BALZAC, *A Harlot High and Low*

7. The third London

Figure 53: the spatial system of *Our Mutual Friend*. As the caption shows, one of the book's earliest scenes – Eugene's and Mor-

53. *Our Mutual Friend*

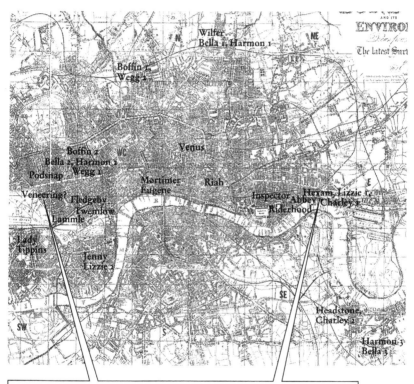

The wheels rolled on, and rolled down by the Monument and by the Tower, and by the Docks; down by Ratcliffe, and by Rotherhithe; down by where accumulated scum of humanity seemed to be washed from higher grounds, like so much moral sewage, and to be pausing until its own weight forced it over the bank and sunk it into the river. [...] the wheels rolled on, until they stopped at a dark corner, river-washed and otherwise not washed at all, where the boy alighted and opened the door. [...] 'This is a confoundedly out-of-the-way place,' said Mortimer, slipping over the stones ...

CHARLES DICKENS, *Our Mutual Friend*, 3

timer's long coach ride from the West End to Limehouse – conveys right away Dickens' stroke of genius: to unify the two halves of London. To see the city as a whole, as a single system. And Dickens succeeds because he too comes up with a 'story of the Third' of sorts; in the sense that between the West End of silver-fork novels, and the East End of Newgate novels, he inserts *a third London*: a sort of wedge, that holds the two extremes together. The details are all different from Balzac's, by all means – but it's significant that the first two great city novelists should hit upon the same basic design, the same triangular *Bauplan* for their narrative. Dickens' Third, then, is the London in the middle of figure 53, like Mortimer and Eugene, who live indeed at the center of town, and receive visits from all parts of London (Boffin, Charley, Headstone, Riderhood, Mr Wren). And the same is true of Riah (Jenny, Lizzie, Fledgeby, Twemlow), and even of the grim Mr Venus; not to mention the more or less random encounters that occur in the streets (Harmon and Boffin, Headstone and Eugene, Boffin and Venus, Eugene and Riah . . .), and again, usually, near the center of town.

Think of this pattern in the light of *Oliver Twist* (figure 39): between the two books, Dickens' characters have realized a *Reconquista* of the City from the underworld (in a symbolic movement that duplicates the dismantling of the 'rookeries' of central London). And in a sense the process begins precisely in *Oliver Twist*, where Fagin and his associates are driven further and further east as the novel proceeds: from the initial den in Field Lane, near Saffron Hill, to the Whitechapel one ('a full half hour' east of Smithfield), then to Sikes' abode in Bethnal Green (where Nancy is killed), and finally to Jacob's Island (to the south-east of the Tower), where Sikes ends up killing himself.

So, the City had already been 'liberated' in *Oliver Twist*. But it had also remained *completely empty*: no more criminals, to be sure, but no one else either (when the Maylies arrive in London, they set up house near the park, and Mr Brownlow, initially in Pentonville, also moves towards the West End). Why this eerie void, this hole right in the middle of London? Probably because the West/East polarization was so powerful – on the social plane, on the moral one, and also, as we have seen, on the narrative level – the binary conception of London was so powerful that Dickens *quite literally did not know what to do with this third space in the middle*: the excluded middle, indeed. Then, one piece at a time, he begins to 'settle' it: the Cheerybles brothers in *Nicholas Nickleby*, Mrs Todgers and the Temple in *Martin Chuzzlewit*, the Gills–Dombey axis in *Dombey and Son* ... And gradually, the third London that had initially served a wholly subordinate function – a mere link between the much more significant extremes of Poverty and Wealth: like Mortimer and Eugene in that opening scene of *Our Mutual Friend* – this third London acquires an autonomous, and in fact a *dominant* narrative role. Because this London is, quite simply, the world of the English middle class (figures 54 and 55).

The middle class: Dickens' Third. But what does it mean, here, being the Third? First of all, it means being surrounded by hostile forces. *Our Mutual Friend* is caught between the fraudulent arrogance of the West End and the physical violence of the Docks, where the mutual friend is indeed almost killed. Arthur Clennam is trapped between a banker's unfathomable speculations and the debtor's prison; Pip, between Estella's upper-class cynicism and the underworld's life-and-death struggle; David Copperfield, between Steerforth's shallow seductiveness and Heep's ambitious hypocrisy. The symmetry is not really perfect – as we will see in a minute – but as a first sketch this will do. Dickens' middle class is indeed *a class in the middle*: encircled by villains, East and West.[18]

What is to be done, then? Keep a distance from London, is Dickens' reply: work in the City, and in the evening leave for the suburbs – like Nicholas Nickleby, John Carker, Wilfer, Harmon, Tom Pinch, Mr Morfin ... A real historical trend, clearly enough; but transmuted by Dickens into a symbolic paradigm which elevates the middle class

---

[18] Could we even speak of a middle class, in Dickens, *if it weren't for its position*? What does a garbage collector have in common with a barrister, or a restorer of skeletons with a housewife, or a doll-dressmaker with a bank clerk? Almost nothing. But in Dickens, they all share the same topographical position at the center of London: halfway between the West End of the élite, and the manual wage labourers to the East and the South.

54. The third London

Dickens' middle class occupies a triangle loosely comprised between Islington, the City, and Soho. Many of these characters work in the City and live north of it (Holborn, Pentonville, Camden Town, Holloway), although in several cases (especially in the legal professions) work and home coincide.

Novels included: *Oliver Twist, Nicholas Nickleby, Martin Chuzzlewit, Dombey and Son, David Copperfield, Bleak House, Great Expectations, A Tale of Two Cities, Little Dorrit, Our Mutual Friend*

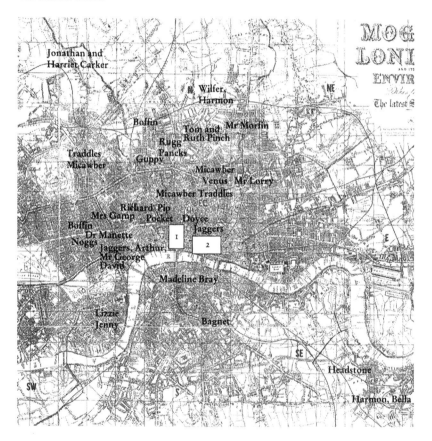

1. Inns of Court and vicinity

   Eugene, Mortimer, Mr Tulkinghorn, Nemo, Mr Snagsby, David Copperfield, Vholes, Ada, Richard C., Tom Pinch, John Westlock, Pip, Sidney Carton

2. The City

   Solomon Gills, Walter Gay, Mrs Todgers, Jonas Chuzzlewit, Cheerybles Brothers, Tim Linkinwater, Nicholas Nickleby, Pip, Doyce and Clennam, Riah, Lizzie, Wilfer

55. Movements of four Dickens heroes

The map indicates the residences of Oliver Twist, David Copperfield, Pip, and Arthur Clennam. Their space overlaps almost entirely with the middle-class wedge of figure 54, except for Oliver's and Arthur's downward mobility (Oliver dragged eastwards into Whitechapel, and Arthur imprisoned in the Marshalsea, south of the Thames). It would be hard to find here a spatial equivalent of Balzac's relentless 'orientation' of Paris along the axis of desire: apart from Little Dorrit, who lives in the Marshalsea, all women desired by these young men live outside of London: Estella in Richmond, Pet in Twickenham, Dora Spenlow in Norwood (and, one may add, Steerforth in Highgate).

Dickens had himself lived in the London inhabited by his heroes (especially Oliver Twist): in Furnival's Inn, in 1836, and Doughty Street (1837–39). However, the two residences where he spent most of his time (Devonshire Terrace and Tavistock Square: where he lived from 1839 to 1851, and from 1851 to 1860) are much closer to the execrated West End.

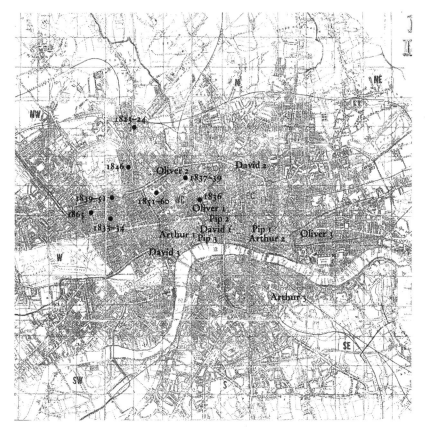

• Dickens' residences in London

above all other social groups (and in fact, above the social universe altogether). The laborers of Took's Court, I mean, or of Bleeding Heart Yard, or of Limehouse, work and live in the very same place; and the same is true of the West End, where residence and workplace are virtually interchangeable (if one can speak of 'work' for Dickens' élite).[19] At London's two extremes, in other words, *life and labor coincide*: social classification – *class* – is always unmistakably present. But in the middle, the work/home dialectics allows Dickens' middle class to have truly *two lives*: a public one in the workplace – and a private one at home. A social existence, or perhaps a social 'mask' in the City, like Wemmick in *Great Expectations*: and then at Walworth, in the suburb, at home, a truer *moral existence* (figure 56).

How different everything is from Balzac, with his movement not so much between work and home, but rather between work-and-home, on the one hand, *and the world of desire on the other*. The initial diagnosis is similar, in both novelists: urban life is hard, artificial, complicated, and requires some relief. But then, Balzac's characters plunge even deeper into the urban maelstrom: they run to their lover, go to the Opéra and the Palais Royal, gamble till dawn; whereas Dickens' characters withdraw to the counter-world of the suburb, to protect their moral illusions. And as for the capital city, so for the nation as a whole. Figure 45 showed the relationship between Paris and France in the *Comédie*: a centripetal pull from which no one escapes (Lucien, who runs away in despair, and wants to drown in the river of his native Charente, is recaptured by Jacques Collin, and taken back to Paris: so he hangs himself in a jail cell). By contrast, Dickens' London has almost no gravitational force: everybody runs away (except scoundrels). Even the rare exceptions confirm the general pattern: David Copperfield and Agnes will probably settle in London, but their love has blossomed elsewhere, between

---

[19] In *Our Mutual Friend*, Wilfer works as a clerk for Veneering (in Mincing Lane, in the City), and we see him in his office as well as in the private settings of Holloway, Greenwich, and Blackheath. Veneering, on the other hand (or Podsnap, or Merdle), exists only in the West End – although he probably goes to the City every day of the week. Significantly, the only upper class character of *Our Mutual Friend* that shows up in the City (Fledgeby) does so *incognito*, pretending to be an acquaintance of Riah's, rather than the pawnshop's real owner.

56. Dickens' Greater London

The growth of London in the course of the nineteenth century implied the rapid absorption of many villages within an urban continuum. Many of Dickens' characters (very often the best ones) live however in the villages that have not yet been completely incorporated, or lie at the edge of the urban system.

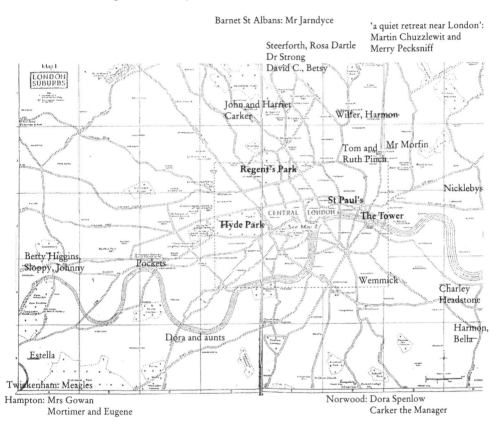

Barnet St Albans: Mr Jarndyce

'a quiet retreat near London': Martin Chuzzlewit and Merry Pecksniff

Steerforth, Rosa Dartle
Dr Strong
David C., Betsy

John and Harriet Carker

Wilfer, Harmon

Tom and Ruth Pinch · Mr Morfin

Regent's Park

Nicklebys

St Paul's

Hyde Park

The Tower

Betty Higgins, Sloppy, Johnny

Pockets

Wemmick

Charley Headstone

Dora and aunts

Harmon, Bella

Estella

Twickenham: Meagles

Hampton: Mrs Gowan
Mortimer and Eugene

Norwood: Dora Spenlow
Carker the Manager

In the suburb one might live and die without marring the image of an innocent world, except when some shadow of its evil fell over a column in the newspaper. Thus the suburb served as an asylum for the preservation of illusion. Here domesticity could flourish, forgetful of the exploitation on which so much of it was based. Here individuality could prosper, oblivious of the pervasive regimentation beyond. This was not merely a child-centered environment: it was based on a childish view of the world, in which reality was sacrificed to the pleasure principle.

LEWIS MUMFORD, *The City in History*

Canterbury and Dover. After years of aimless London encounters, Lizzie and Eugene finally get married – in a countryside inn (figure 57). And here are the endings of *Old Goriot* and *Little Dorrit*:

> Left alone, Rastignac walked a few steps to the highest part of the cemetery, and saw Paris spread out below on both banks of the winding Seine. Lights were beginning to twinkle here and there. His gaze fixed almost avidly upon the space that lay between the column of the Place Vendôme and the dome of the Invalides; there lay the splendid world that he had wished to conquer. He eyed that humming hive with a look that foretold its despoliation, as if he already felt on his lips the sweetness of its honey, and said with superb defiance: 'It's war, between us two!'.
>
> And as the first act of his challenge to society Rastignac went to dine with Madame de Nucingen.

> They all gave place when the signing was done, and Little Dorrit and her husband walked out of the church alone. They paused for a moment on the steps of the portico, looking at the fresh perspective of the street in the autumn morning sun's bright rays, and then went down.
>
> Went down into a modest life of usefulness and happiness. Went down to give a mother's care, in the fullness of time, to Fanny's neglected children no less than their own, and to leave that lady going into Society for ever and a day. Went down to give a tender nurse and friend to Tip for some few years [. . .] They went quietly down into the roaring streets, inseparable and blessed; and as they passed along in sunshine and shade, the noisy and the eager, and the arrogant and the froward and the vain, fretted and chafed, and made their usual uproar.

We are in London, here – but why? By mere narrative inertia, it seems. Fanny and Arthur have no *desire* to be there, and their activities are hardly urban ones (if anything, they suggest a rural, extended family). London, for its part, is stupid, arrogant, grotesque, aggressive – but can be easily avoided: it exists 'around', or better still *outside* the characters, not *in* them, like Rastignac's Paris. Fanny and Arthur are untouched, innocent: 'in' London, perhaps, but not 'of' it. Personally, I see them in the suburbs.

57. A geography of Dickens' endings

A very large number of characters leave London at the end of Dickens' novels: sometimes because they are practically sent into exile, but more often because the urban experience has been so devastating that London cannot provide a plausible setting for the happy ending.

By contrast, London is the elective abode of most villains, the upper class in full ranks, and social climbers like Claypole and Heep. The number of characters who die in London – or perhaps 'of' London, like many in *Bleak House* (Richard, Miss Flite, the man from Shropshire, Krook, Hawdon, Jo, Lady Dedlock, Mr Tulkinghorn) – is also extremely high.

1. Betty Higgins, Headstone,
   Lizzie, Eugene, Riderhood
2. Maylies, Mr Brownlow, Oliver
3. Dr Losberne, Mr Grimwig
4. Joe, Biddy
5. Nicholas Nickleby, Madeline,
   Kate, Mrs Nickleby, Noggs
? 'in the country': John Westlock,
   Ruth, Tom Pinch, Martin
   Chuzzlewit, Mary Graham

Woodcourt, Esther

Mr George

C. Bates

Mr Jarndyce

? Mark Tapley

to 'distant parts of the new world': Monks
'abroad': Lammles
India: Maldon
France: Sir Mulberry Hawk, Veneerings
Italy: Edith Dombey
Cairo: Pip, Matthew Pocket
Australia: Micawber, Mell, Peggotty, Little Emily, Martha
Tasmania: Augustus Moddle
USA: Mr Crummles

8. *Very Curiously Brought Together*

What can I do, I like Balzac better than Dickens, forgive me. There is one issue, however – the narrative presentation of the city – on which Dickens was actually more radical than his French contemporary. Return to figure 41, the Paris of *Lost Illusions*. A 'mythic' sociology, Walter Benjamin wrote; the first novel of complexity; the first story of the Third; for me, the greatest novel ever written. And yet, Balzac's presentation of Paris is quite elementary: the city takes shape through Lucien's movements, one space at a time, one step after the other (and with a lot of explanations by the narrator). It is a linear, uncomplicated course, where the reader is on very safe ground, and has no efforts to make.

And now, the London of *Our Mutual Friend*: figures 58*a–h*, that follow its first eight monthly installments, from May to December 1864. Look at the rhythm of this narrative pattern: with every new installment, always one or two new spaces; and then, unlike *Lost Illusions*, a plot that doesn't move in an orderly way from one space to the next, but *jumps* – and then jumps again: from the Thames to the

---

58*a–h*

The eight maps indicate the gradual unfolding of London in *Our Mutual Friend*. Each map corresponds to one of the first eight monthly parts published by Chapman and Hall; and with each new part, as can clearly be seen, Dickens takes care to introduce some new spaces, with new characters, and (often) new social features. By December 1864 (map 58*h*: roughly halfway through the book), the novel's spatial system is virtually complete; from then on, narrative novelty no longer depends directly on spatial novelty, but rather on interactions among the different spaces.

I have already mentioned the social gulf opened (and bridged) in the first three chapters of the novel (the Thames; the West End; Limehouse). But if the novel opens with a look at the two social extremes, the sequence of maps highlights the progressive centrality of the middle classes in Dickens' urban system, beginning with the Wilfers (58*a*), Wegg and Venus (58*b*), Boffin, Eugene and Mortimer (58*c*). If one looks at the East–West dominant of the first installment, and compares it to the network of the eighth one, the middle-class 'wedge' leaps to the eye.

● new space ▶ new meeting
◉ previously mentioned space ▷ previously mentioned meeting

58a. *Our Mutual Friend*, May 1864

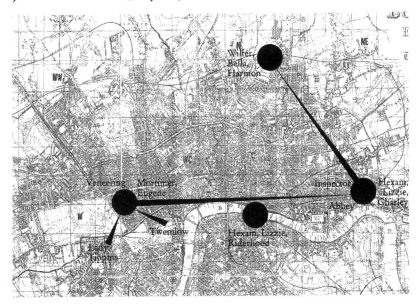

58b. *Our Mutual Friend*, June 1864

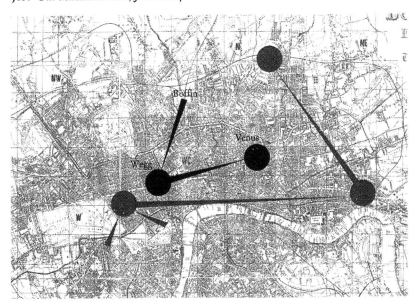

58c.   Our Mutual Friend, July 1864

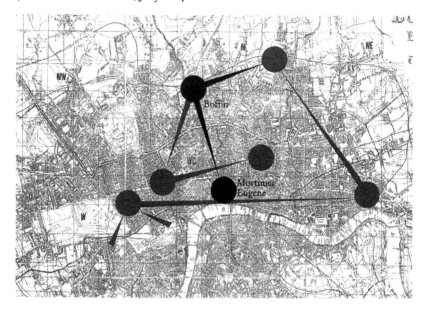

58d.   Our Mutual Friend, August 1864

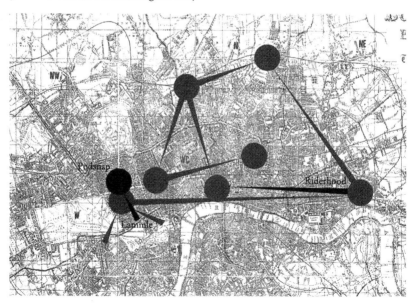

58e. *Our Mutual Friend*, September 1864

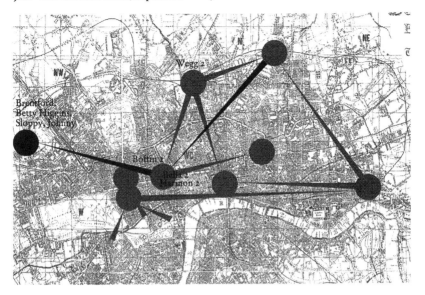

58f. *Our Mutual Friend*, October 1864

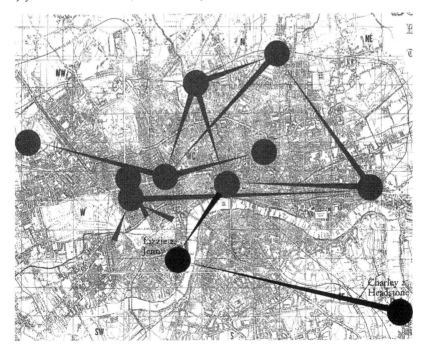

58g. *Our Mutual Friend*, November 1864

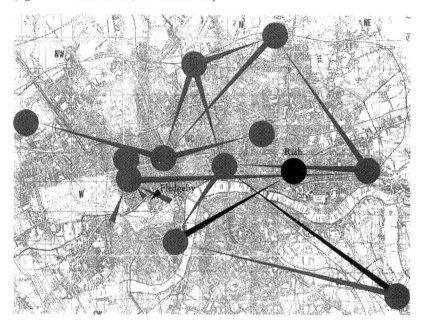

58h. *Our Mutual Friend*, December 1864

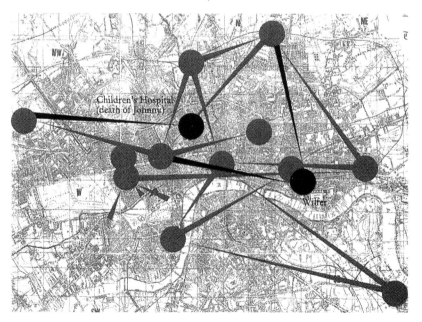

West End, to Limehouse, to Holloway, to Wegg's lonely street corner . . . Fantastic idea: the city – *the generalized spatial proximity unique to the city* – as a genuine enigma: a 'mosaic of worlds', yes, but whose tiles have been randomly scattered. Raymond Williams, *The Country and the City*:

> As we stand and look back at a Dickens novel the general movement we remember [. . .] is a hurrying seemingly random passing of men and women, each heard in some fixed phrase, seen in some fixed expression: a way of seeing men and women that belongs to the street. There is at first an absence of ordinary connection and development . . .[20]

An absence of connections, at the beginning. Then the plot unfolds, and those unrelated spaces are linked in the increasingly intricate web of the maps in figure 58. But linked by what, exactly? Williams again:

> But then as the action develops, unknown and unacknowledged relationships, profound and decisive connections, definite and committing recognitions and avowals are as it were forced into consciousness.

Profound, decisive, definite, committing . . . Too many adjectives, and too solemn: as if Williams were somewhat embarrassed by what he is describing. And understandably so, because these 'unacknowledged relationships' and 'decisive connections' being 'forced into consciousness' as 'committing recognitions' – these are Dickens' notorious family romances. Sir Leicester Dedlock and Esther Summerson are 'the two last persons on earth I should have thought of connecting together!', exclaims Mr Jarndyce (*Bleak House*, 43). And elsewhere in the same novel:

> What connexion can there be, between the place in Lincolnshire, the house in town, the Mercury in powder, and the whereabouts of Jo the outlaw with the broom, who had that distant ray of light upon him when he swept the churchyard-step? What connexion can there have been between many people in the innumerable histories of this world, who, from opposite sides of great gulfs, have, nevertheless, been very curiously brought together!
> *Bleak House*, 16

[20] Raymond Williams, *The Country and the City*, Oxford University Press, 1973, pp. 154–5.

What connexion? Always the same, in *Oliver Twist* and *Nicholas Nickleby*, *Bleak House*, *Great Expectations*, *Little Dorrit*, *Our Mutual Friend*: a bloodline. Lost and disavowed children, secret loves of the past, missing and stolen and insane wills: all acts that have *separated* into the many urban sub-systems the family that now the novel brings together again. Time after time, the family romance acts thus as Dickens' fundamental scaffold, whose structuring power is never equaled by the plot's sociological axis (not even at its most intense: say, Merdle's bankruptcy in *Little Dorrit*). It is a further instance of the tentative, contradictory path followed by urban novels: as London's random and unrelated enclaves increase the 'noise', the dissonance, the complexity of the plot – the family romance tries to *reduce* it, turning London into a coherent whole. A composite and precarious formal system thus comes into being, suspended between the isolated city sketch (which was of course Dickens' initial form), and a biographical fairy-tale that tries, in one way or another, to establish a unity.

That tries to establish a unity . . . Still, take figures 59–61, where Dickens' three great London novels are segmented along the same lines as *Lost Illusions* and *Sentimental Education* (figures 50, 51). In Dickens, the wide central overlap so typical of Parisian novels – after all, *isn't the city precisely a center?* – has shrunk almost to nothing, and what little is left is occupied by spoiled, lazy figures like Mortimer and Eugene, or the inept dreamer Arthur Clennam of *Little Dorrit*. (*Bleak House*, of course, is the exception: but the central space of the Law – except for Bucket, all scoundrels, madmen, or corpses – is a slaughterhouse, not a place to inhabit.) As if they were a set of narrative X-rays, these diagrams show us London as an archipelago of autonomous 'villages' (Twickenham, Bleeding Heart Yard, the Marshalsea, the West End . . .), where the various novelistic threads remain largely unrelated. And when the various social groups do indeed come into contact, it's striking how everything stays on a strictly *personal* level: Lizzie's love affair with Eugene doesn't force her to face the West End's snobbish cruelty – nor force Eugene to confront the world of manual labor and chronic want.

Whereas Balzac's characters *change* class (if they are very strong, and very lucky), Dickens' seem rather to *transcend* it, landing in an enchanted realm where all relationships are ethical ones, and the *milieu* – the 'demonic form' taken by social relations, as Auerbach writes in *Mimesis* – has lost all its power.[21]

[21] Significantly enough, *milieu* has no real English equivalent, and the French term (according to the OED) was first used by a British writer in 1877, seven years after Dickens' death.

---

59. *Our Mutual Friend*
The different sections of this diagram, and of those that follow, constitute largely autonomous narrative universes: each of them complete with villains, innocent victims, comic characters, mysteries, melodramatic possibilities. Such ingredients are however unevenly distributed in the text: villains are much more abundant in the West End, for instance, while certain kinds of 'virtuous' interaction tend to happen more frequently between the middle class and the laboring poor (see below, figure 62).

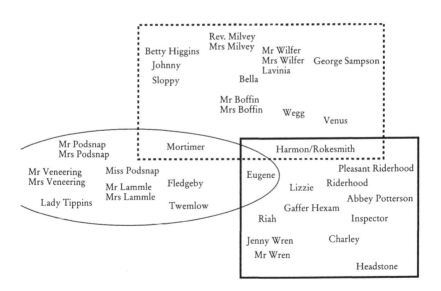

And indeed, look at the pattern emerging from figure 62: the upper class as a minor appendix, and that intense flow between middle and lower classes. It's Dickens' petty bourgeois utopia: the Third, the class in the middle, as the hinge of the social system, and its main source of value. No more devouring ambition to 'make it' at whatever cost, as in the French (and Russian) middle class, but only the modest hope for a decent and laborious life, open to the best elements of the proletariat – where 'best' indicates, again, a total lack of ambition. In this pious travesty of the relationship between ethics and success, social mobility is granted only to the meek: Little

60. *Little Dorrit*

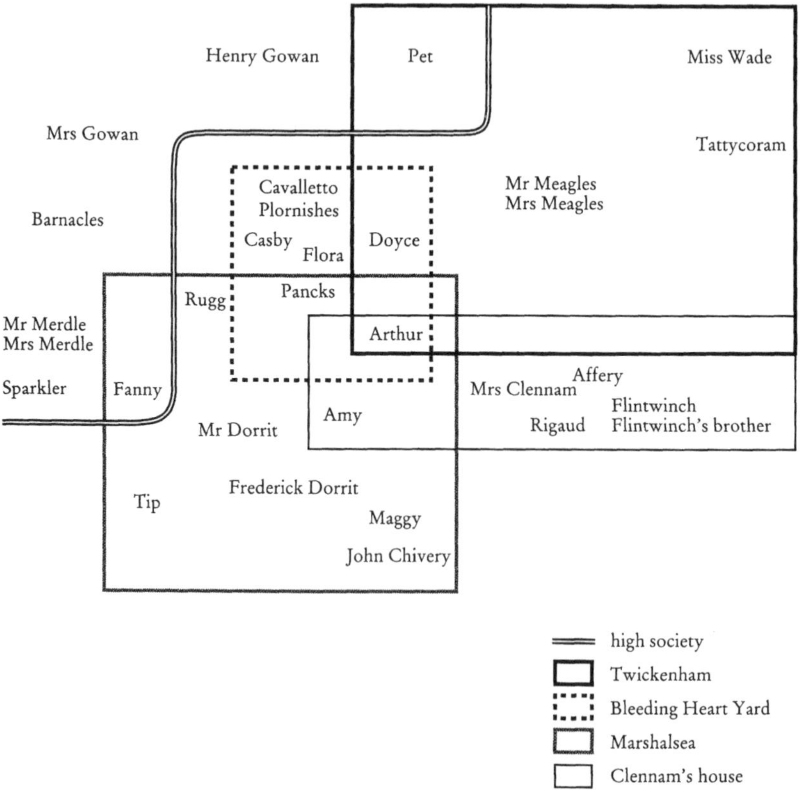

high society
Twickenham
Bleeding Heart Yard
Marshalsea
Clennam's house

Dorrit, Charley and Esther in *Bleak House*, Lizzie, Jenny, Sloppy, Bella Wilfer after her regeneration, and of course those wonderful Boffins. The only dissonance is those greedy relatives that would be unpresentable in such a virtuous world (Hexam, Riderhood, Mr Wren, Mr Dorrit, Tip . . .), and who are consequently slaughtered *en masse* so that the happy ending may be. But they bring it upon themselves, and it is really nobody's fault.

61. *Bleak House*

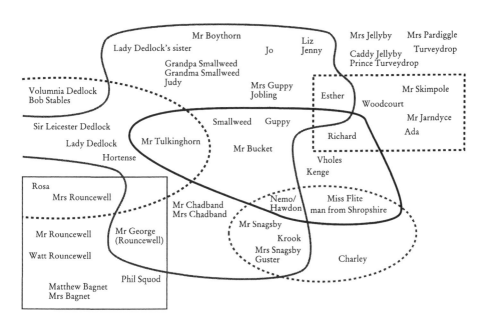

9. *City of clues*

Dickens' London. And Conan Doyle's – just as legendary, in its own way. And so, while working at the maps that follow, I conducted among friends and colleagues a little poll about Holmes' city. The answers were all very firm: fog, the East End, blind alleys, the Docks, the Thames, the Tower . . .

Figure 63: Sherlock Holmes' London. A small cluster of crimes in the City, a few more here and there; but the epicenter is clearly in the West End. The working class areas lying south of the Thames, so prominent in Doyle's first two novels ('Larkhall Lane. Stockwell Place. Robert Street. Coldharbour Lane. Our quest does not appear to take us to very fashionable regions': *The Sign of Four*) have practically disappeared; and as for the East End, Holmes goes there exactly once in fifty-six stories.

---

62. *Our Mutual Friend*, encounters across class lines

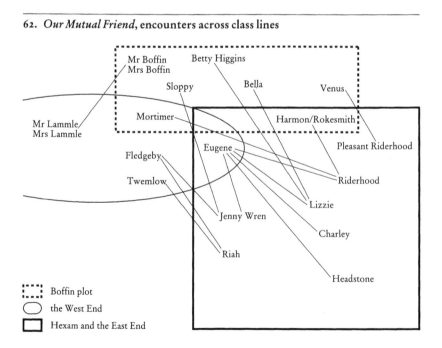

63. Sherlock Holmes' London

Unlike Doyle's first two novels, which take place mostly south of the Thames, between Lambeth and Camberwell, the short stories published in the *Strand Magazine* from 1891 onwards focus almost entirely on the West End and the City.

As the early novels were not very successful, whereas the short stories were immediately extremely popular, Holmes may well owe his success to this shift in location, with which Doyle 'guessed' the right space for detective fiction.

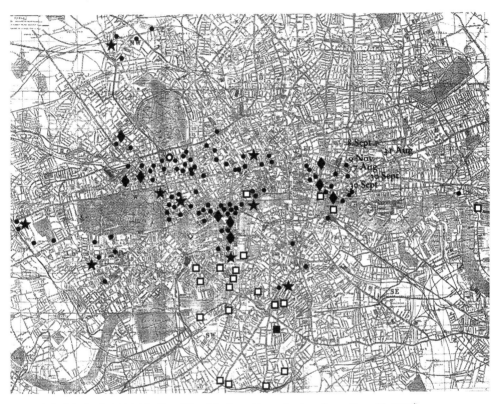

A Study in Scarlet (1887), *The Sign of Four* (1890):

■ murders (not shown: Upper Norwood)
□ Holmes' movements

short stories (1891–1927):

O 221B Baker Street
● Holmes' movements
★ murders
◆ other crimes
7 Aug etc.: Jack the Ripper murders

'I'm afraid,' said Holmes, smiling, 'that all the queen's horses and all the queen's men cannot avail in this matter.' He had spread out his big map of London and leaned eagerly over it.

'Well, well,' said he presently with an exclamation of satisfaction, 'things are turning a little in our direction at last. Why, Watson, I do honestly believe that we are going to pull it off, after all.'

ARTHUR CONAN DOYLE, *The Adventure of the Bruce-Partington Plan*

And now, look at figure 64: the 'vicious, semi-criminal' areas of Booth's London map. It is the exact inverse of Doyle's city of crime. There are some minor clusters of 'dangerous classes' in Paddington, Westminster, Soho, Camden Town; but the area of maximum concentration begins near the Tower, and then stretches east, between Bethnal Green and Whitechapel, in the areas of greatest urban misery.

In other words: *fictional crime in the London of wealth*; *real crime, in the London of poverty*. The asymmetry may well have begun for 'tactical' reasons: Doyle is forging the myth of the omniscient detective, and it would be unwise to let him go near Jack the Ripper's Whitechapel (and as figure 63 shows, if Holmes finds himself in that area, he quickly turns around). But apart from this, there

---

64. Charles Booth's dangerous classes

The map indicates the areas of greatest density for the lowest social group – 'Vicious. Semi-criminal' – included in Booth's 1889 'Descriptive Map of London Poverty'.

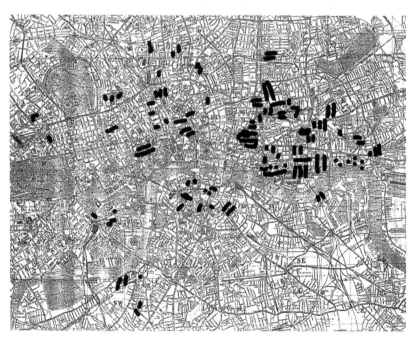

is a deep symbolic logic behind those two Londons. Booth's criminal world is the nearly inevitable result of urban poverty: it is a visible, widespread reality, which has absolutely no mystery about it. For detective fiction, however, crime must be precisely an *enigma*: an unheard-of event, a 'case', an 'adventure'. And these things require a very different setting from the East End: they need fancy hotels, mansions overlooking the park, great banks, diplomatic secrets . . . It's the old London of privilege, that we encounter in detective fiction: the same streets, the same houses and squares of silver-fork novels. In Booth's map, Baker Street is bright red, surrounded by a sea of gold.

London. And then the rural adventures of figure 65 – that seldom, however, take us very far from the city. Doyle's favorite counties are Surrey, Kent, Sussex (where the aging Holmes retires to tend bees): code words for a weekend in the country, suggests Francis Mulhern, who is certainly right.[22] And this world of parks and country houses and estates cannot help but recall – of all the maps we have seen so far – the very first one: Austen's England. As in her time, England feels threatened, and Doyle's contemporaries invent the unbelievable form of 'invasion literature': dozens of extremely popular novels where the French, the Germans, the Russians (and eventually also Wells' Martians) land in the south of England, and march on the capital (whereas Dracula, in his superior wisdom, lands in the North-East). Michael Matin, who has studied this forgotten genre in depth, has produced a map that so closely recalls Holmes' England (figure 66) that the crimes occurring south of London (all murders) begin to look like Doyle's trope for a foreign invasion. Which is after all not

---

[22] Similar reflections in a recent study by Loïc Ravenel: 'Within Holmes' world, the countryside is first and foremost a space which is attached to the city. [. . .] The physical connection is established by the railway, and by a network of urban and rural train stations. [. . .] The rapidity of the means of communication situates the universe of the countryside in the proximity of the city. Characters can reach it at all times, easily, and in fact with a certain amount of pleasure. Distances, calculated in units of time, have been reduced to almost nothing. In conclusion, the countryside is for all practical purposes a mere appendix of the urban context' (Loïc Ravenel, *Les Aventures géographiques de Sherlock Holmes*, Découvrir, Paris 1994, pp. 202–3).

65. Murder in the countryside

As Holmes moves away from London, crimes have a marked tendency to become bloodier. In the city, less than half of his cases have to do with violent death; in the countryside, the percentage of murders (or attempted murders) rises to three-quarters. In the first Holmes collection – the *Adventures* – the contrast of city and countryside was even starker, as none of the seven London stories involved murder, while all of the five countryside ones did. Then, murder became *de rigueur* for detective fiction, and Doyle must have tried to combine it with the urban setting. Given the much greater charm of the earlier, bloodless London stories (*A Scandal in Bohemia*, *The Red-Headed League*, *The Man with the Twisted Lip*), maybe it wasn't such a good idea.

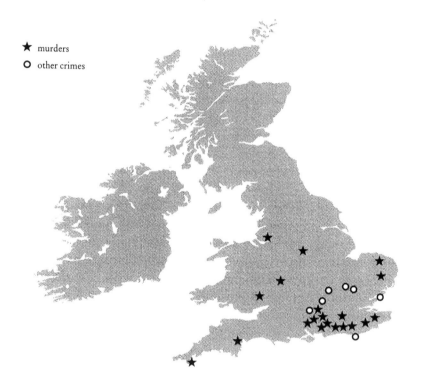

★ murders
O other crimes

'Good Heavens!' I cried. 'Who would associate crime with these dear old homesteads?'

'They always fill me with a certain horror. It is my belief, Watson, founded upon my experience, that the lowest and vilest alleys in London do not present a more dreadful record of sin than does the smiling and beautiful countryside.'

'You horrify me!'

ARTHUR CONAN DOYLE, *The Adventure of the Copper Beeches*

66. Geography of 'invasion literature' (1871–1906)

Novels included: Colonel George Chesney, *The Battle of Dorking* (1871); 'Grip', *How John Bull Lost London* (1882); Horace Francis Lester, *The Taking of Dover* (1888); William Le Queux, *The Great War of 1897* (1894); Colonel F.N. Maude, *The Second Battle of Dorking* (1900); T.W. Offin, *How the Germans Took London* (1900); 'General Staff', *The Writing on the Wall* (1906); William Le Queux, *The Invasion of 1910* (1906)

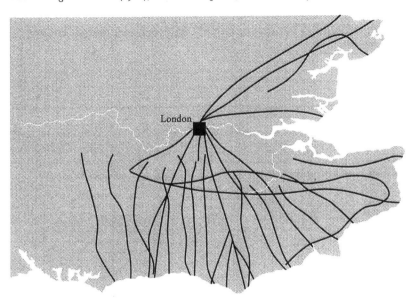

—— Route followed by the French, German and Russian troops

You ask me to tell you, my grand-children, something about my own share in the great events that happened fifty years ago. 'Tis sad work to turn back to that bitter page in our history, but you may perhaps take profit in your new homes from the lessons it teaches. For us in England it came too late. And yet we had plenty of warnings, if we had only made use of them. The danger did not come on us unawares. It burst on us suddenly, 'tis true, but its coming was foreshadowed plainly enough to open our eyes, if we had not been wilfully blind. We English have only ourselves to blame for the humiliation which has been brought on the land. Venerable old age! Dishonourable old age, I say, when it follows a manhood dishonoured as ours has been...

COLONEL G.T. CHESNEY, *The Battle of Dorking; Being an Account of the German Invasion of England, as Told by a Volunteer to his Grandchildren*

unlikely in a narrative universe where almost half of the criminals are foreigners (figure 67), and where in the *only* story which is set outside England – *The Final Problem*, at the sources of the Rhine – Sherlock Holmes is immediately killed (but he comes back to life: in Park Lane . . .)

'How England became an island', Braudel once wrote. Indeed.

---

67. 'Rache'

Unlike the French villains of figure 10, Doyle's foreign criminals are mostly from the United States, Germany, and Italy: the sign of new economic (USA) and politico-military (Germany) rivalries that have replaced the old Anglo–French antagonism. As for Italy, its presence in early detective fiction is usually motivated by Mafia-like secret societies.

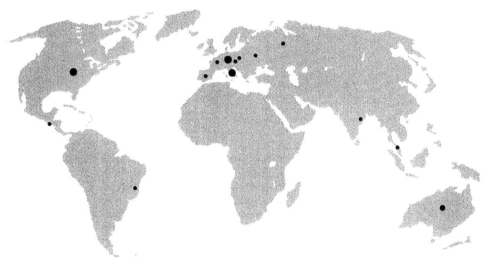

• country of foreign
  criminal

In rapid succession we passed through the fringe of fashionable London, hotel London, theatrical London, literary London, commercial London, and, finally, maritime London, till we came to a riverside city of a hundred thousand souls, where the tenement houses swelter and reek with the outcasts of Europe . . .

ARTHUR CONAN DOYLE, *The Adventure of the Six Napoleons*

Chapter 3
Narrative markets, ca. 1850

Narrative markets: sociology of literature, as it used to be called; history of the book, history of reading, as we call it nowadays. It is a new field, growing, full of surprises: that however hasn't yet really bitten into literary history, and even less into morphological study. There is great diplomacy between book historians and literary historians, but true intellectual engagement is still to come. So, the first aim of this chapter is to build a bridge between two lines of research: book history – and the history of forms. They seem very distant; they *are* very distant. And that's why the bridge is useful.

Then, this chapter tries to be a *quantitative* study: 'serial history of the third level' (the level of culture), as Pierre Chaunu has once called it.[1] As in all serial history, my object is an artificial one, because a series is never 'found', but always constructed – and constructed by focusing on what is *repeatable* and can therefore turn discrete objects into a series. And this, of course, is what makes quantitative methods so repugnant to literary critics: the fear that they may suppress the uniqueness of texts. Which indeed they do. But as I don't believe in the epistemological value of the unique, its suppression doesn't really bother me, and in fact... But of this, more later.

Finally, of course, this is also a chapter of cultural geography. Book historians have already shown that the literary market is 'vertically' divided, among different social groups; here, I study its

---

[1] Pierre Chaunu, 'Un nouveau champ pour l'histoire sérielle: le quantitatif au troisième niveau', in *Méthodologie de l'histoire et des sciences humaines*, Privat, Toulouse 1973.

'horizontal' divisions, among different places. Which will force me to reflect on the many spaces of literary history – provinces, nation, continent, planet . . . – and on the hierarchy that binds them together.

I

1. 'Experiments upon diagrams'

Figure 68: British circulating libraries of the mid nineteenth century. At that time, most readers did not buy novels, but borrowed them from these widespread commercial establishments, which are therefore excellent indicators of the Victorian cultural market. Unfortunately, however, although we have many catalogues of these libraries, no loan records have survived:[2] in other words, we know what books were on the shelves, but not whether they were read or not. Still, this major limitation makes a study of what was on the market even more significant: if we cannot know what people *did* actually read, finding out what they *could* (or could *not*) read is really all we can do.

In 1993, then, after having consulted some book historians, I wrote to several British libraries, and ended up with the 14 catalogues of figure 68. As the catalogues arrange books alphabetically, I took the first hundred titles of each collection, in order to have comparable random samples, and started to study them. With a very simple hope: that I would find *a lot of unevenness*. Geography thrives on unevenness (if rivers, mountains, cities were evenly distributed everywhere, maps would be pointless, and geography wouldn't exist); and then, I have always been skeptical about the concept of national literature, and was counting on unevenness to dis-integrate it into an archipelago of separate circuits: the markets, plural, that give this chapter its title.

---

[2] With one exception, which is the object of an excellent study by Jan Fergus, 'Eighteenth-Century Readers in Provincial England: The Customers of Samuel Clay's Circulating Library and Bookshop in Warwick, 1770–72', *The Papers of the Bibliographical Society of America*, vol. 78, no. 2, 1984.

I had my samples; and I had to analyze them. But how? For me, the ideal analytical unit would be genre: but the taxonomy of nineteenth-century narrative is such a disaster, and many titles in these catalogues are so obscure that – for the time being – a full generic breakdown was out of the question. So I measured the up-to-dateness of the various collections, but didn't find much. Next, I turned to a third indicator, which was, loosely speaking, a measure of 'canonicity': how many of the hundred novels in each sample had been written by authors listed in the *Dictionary of National*

---

68. Circulating libraries 1838–61

Catalogues consulted: Ebers' (London 1838), Literary Society (Madras 1839), Lovejoy's (Reading 1845), Collumbell's (Derby 1845), Public Library (Norwich 1847), Public Library (Beccles 1847), Hewitt's (Derby 1849), Davies' (Cheltenham 1849), Henriques' (Cheltenham 1849), Kaye's (Newcastle-upon-Tyne 1852), Plowman's (Oxford 1852), Vibert's (Penzance 1855), Athenaeum & Mechanic Institute (Wolverhampton 1856), British Library (London 1861)

not shown: ● Madras

Biography. The DNB is far from perfect, of course (and also much larger than the canon in the strict sense): but it is a rich and plausible index, already used very effectively by Raymond Williams in his 'Social History of English Writers', and more recently by Gaye Tuchman and Nina Fortin in *Edging Women Out*, their sociological study of canon-formation (and canon-exclusion).[3]

To my great satisfaction, the DNB revealed a very wide oscillation: some libraries had as few as 37 percent DNB texts; others, as many as 88 percent. Here was the unevenness I wanted, finally, and so I immediately turned to one of those statistical strategies – correlation – that even an amateur knows something about: explaining one set of data via another.[4] On one axis the DNB presences, on the other the size of the libraries, and figure 69 is the result. Some data deviate, true, but the general trend is clear, and its meaning is also quite clear: the smaller a collection is, the higher the proportion of DNB texts. *The smaller a collection is, the more canonical it is.*[5] It's what Margaret Cohen says of the teaching canon: its rigidity is a function of having so little time to teach it: ten weeks, twelve, fifteen, whatever – always too few to feel free to change much. Well, the same applies to small libraries: they have only ten or twelve shelves, and so they go straight for 'safe' authors. Private libraries of early modern France show a similar pattern: when a household owns only one book (which is often the case, in the seventeenth century), the choice is never random (fiction here, religion there, travels or history

---

[3] Raymond Williams, *The Long Revolution*, 1961, Penguin, Harmondsworth 1971, pp. 254–70; Gaye Tuchman and Nina Fortin, *Edging Women Out*, Yale University Press, New Haven 1989.

[4] Remember Peirce's words quoted in the *Introduction*: 'operations upon diagrams take the place of experiments upon real things [. . .] *experiments upon diagrams are questions put to the Nature of the relations [of different parts of the diagram to one another]*' (emphasis mine).

[5] It has been pointed out to me that this formulation seems to grant Victorian librarians a prophetic gift of Biblical proportions (figuring out today's canon a century and a half beforehand!). Not so, of course, and the misunderstanding arises out of the mistaken idea that the novelistic canon *is a creation of the school (and the university)*. This is false, it has taken generations for the school to 'accept' the novel, and even then the school merely adopted *those texts that had already been selected by the market* (with a couple of exceptions). If we find today's canon in Victorian commercial libraries, then, it is because they were following the market – just like schools did, a century later.

elsewhere): it is always the same: a devotional work.[6] It is the same principle, really: small size equals safe choices. More cynically: small size equals hegemonic forms: as if these libraries lacked the weight, the critical mass, to withstand the gravitational pull of cultural hegemony. If there is only one book, Religion. And if only one bookcase, the Canon.

A general thesis seems to follow from what I have just said: namely, that size is seldom *just size*. A small library doesn't have the same structure as a large library, only smaller: it has a *different* structure. Different because of the overpowering presence of the canon that we have just seen: and also because something gets lost, when size decreases too much. With respect to foreign literatures, for instance (and although my data show no clear overall trend), one fact seems nevertheless established: in half of the small collections – and only there – translations decrease so much that they virtually disappear: Hewitt's Circulating Library, from Derby, has two foreign

[6] On this, see Roger Chartier, 'Stratégies éditoriales et lectures populaires', in H.-J. Martin and R. Chartier, eds, *Histoire de l'édition française*, vol. I, pp. 585–603.

69. Presence of the canon in British circulating libraries

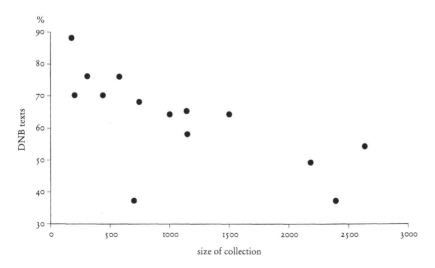

novels in one hundred titles (*Gil Blas*, and *The Mysteries of Paris*); the
Madras Literary Society, one (*Don Quixote*); Vibert's library, at
Penzance, none (figure 70). Here, the change in size has affected the
very structure of the library: less space does not mean *fewer* foreign
novels, but *none at all*. And a library without foreign novels . . . well,
it is a strange creature indeed.

2. *Theoretical interlude IV. Normal literature*

Fine, it has been objected to what I have just said; fine, small collections are hyper-canonical. So what? Basically, this means that
they have all the great books, and don't care about the inferior ones.
And what's wrong with that?

What is wrong is the implicit belief that literature proceeds from
one canonical form to the next, in a sort of unbroken thread. But
modern literature follows a more oblique and discontinuous path:
'canonization of the cadet branch', Viktor Sklovsky liked to call it.
Theory of Prose:

---

70. **Presence of foreign novels in British circulating libraries**

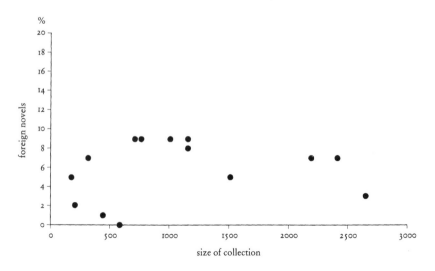

The legacy that is passed on from one literary generation to the next moves not from father to son, but from uncle to nephew [. . .] new literary forms emerge out of the lower stratum of the literary system to replace the old ones [. . .] the vaudeville showman Belopjatkin is reborn as Nekrasov [. . .], Alexander Blok canonizes the themes and rhythms of the 'gypsy song', while Chekhov introduces comic journalism within Russian literature, and Dostoevsky raises the devices of detective fiction to a veritable literary norm.[7]

Vaudeville, gypsies, comic journalism, detective stories; cheap jokes on bureaucrats, and Gogol's *Overcoat*; rough city sketches, and Dickens' London novels; silly colonial adventures, and *Heart of Darkness*; advertising, and *Ulysses* . . . See what happens, when a library confines itself to the canon: by banishing bad literature, it denies its audience the raw material of literary evolution. It becomes scholastic, sterile; the more so, if it also excludes foreign novels. (And one wonders: could it be that the strength of each canon is *directly proportional to the provincialism of its culture?*)

There is then a further theoretical point, of an even more abstract nature. As I said at the beginning, this chapter wants to be (also) a quantitative study: it treats novels wholesale, disregarding their uniqueness. But why should one do that? What is to be gained? What can quantitative methods *add* to the study of literature?

They add, first, a richer historical context. When we read that 'the 18th century [. . .] was the age of the take-off of female literacy *par excellence*',[8] for instance, this strictly quantitative fact helps to explain the growing role of women writers (and readers) for the eighteenth-century novel, and the success of the epistolary form (where literacy is quite directly the central narrative fact), and finally, on a different plane, the stylistic economy – as of one counting on a fully literate audience – displayed by Jane Austen at the turn of the century.

But I am not trying to confine serial history to the extra-literary context; on the contrary, I consider it an excellent model *for the study*

[7] Viktor Sklovsky, *Theory of Prose*, 1929, Dalkey Archive Press, Elmwood Park Ill. 1990, p. 190 (translation slightly modified).

[8] François Furet and Jacques Ozouf, *Reading and Writing. Literacy in France from Calvin to Jules Ferry*, 1977, Cambridge University Press, 1982, p. 37.

of literature itself. Specifically, I have in mind two great achievements of the *Annales* school: the dramatic enlargement of the 'historian's domain', first of all, towards what is everyday, un-monumental, or even invisible (like so many of the novels and writers I found in my catalogues). And then, the related discovery of how *slowly* this territory changes: the discovery of 'histoire immobile', as Braudel has polemically called it.

This is what quantitative methods have to offer to the historian of literature: a reversal of the hierarchy between the exception and the series, where the latter becomes – as it is – the true protagonist of cultural life. A history of literature as history *of norms*, then: a less innovative, much 'flatter' configuration than the one we are used to; repetitive, slow – boring, even. But this is exactly what most of life is like, and instead of redeeming literature from its prosaic features we should learn to recognize them and understand what they mean. Just as most science is 'normal' science – which 'does not aim at novelties [. . .] and, when successful, finds none' – so *most literature is normal literature*: 'mopping up operations', as Kuhn would say: 'an attempt to force [literature] into the preformed and relatively inflexible box that the paradigm supplies.'[9]

A flatter, more boring literature. But then, are we so sure that boredom is boring? Once we learn to confront it, the flatness of literary conventions will appear for the genuine enigma it is. How does a new narrative form crystallize out of a collection of haphazard, half-baked, often horrendous attempts? How does a convention change, or, better: *does* it ever change? Or does it remain stable in a thousand disguises – until the day it suddenly disintegrates? And why does it remain stable so long? And why does it then collapse? And how on earth can the *same* convention work in such *different* places – Scotland and Italy, Denmark and Hungary?

---

[9] Thomas Kuhn, *The Structure of Scientific Revolutions*, 1962, 2nd enlarged edition, Chicago University Press, 1970, pp. 24 and 52. Kuhn's historical dualism (long periods of normal science, and brief bursts of scientific revolutions) is structurally identical to Gould's and Eldredge's theory of 'punctuated equilibria', on whose significance as a historical model for the study of literature I have often insisted.

All questions for another study. Except for the last one, which returns at the end of the chapter.

3. *England becomes an island*

Go back for a moment to the graph that charts the presence of translations in British circulating libraries (figure 70). Size has significant consequences, most likely, but something else is strange here: how few foreign works there are in *all* the collections. Two, three, five, seven, nine percent; but no more, in any of the fourteen libraries. At first these results seemed strange, considering the international circulation of European novels in the nineteenth century, but then they reminded me of an earlier research project on the European novel, conducted with a group of graduate students, at Columbia, in 1992. Back then, we were sampling only three years per century, and basing our investigation almost entirely on the data reported by national bibliographies (that have been put together in the most different ways, and are often unreliable); in absolute terms, therefore, our findings have no definitive value. But when I saw that circulating libraries gave the same results – well, I felt a surge of retrospective trust in our old study; in its *indicative* value, at least.

This, then, is what we found in 1992 for the entire period of the novel's take-off (1750–1850: figure 71), and, more narrowly, for 1816 and 1850 (figure 72). As you can see, most European countries import from abroad a large portion of their novels (40, 50, 60, 80 percent, if not more), whereas France and Britain form a group to themselves, that imports very little from the rest of the European continent: a fact which has a very simple explanation – these two countries *produce* a lot of novels (and good novels, too), so they don't need to buy them abroad. Still, if we narrow our focus, France and Britain prove to have less in common than appears at first sight: whereas in the century of the novel's take-off, France more than doubles its imports, raising them from 10 to over 25 percent (although in 1850 their percentage declines), Britain reduces them regularly with each successive generation, so that the 20 percent of

71. Percentage of foreign novels in European literatures (1750–1850)

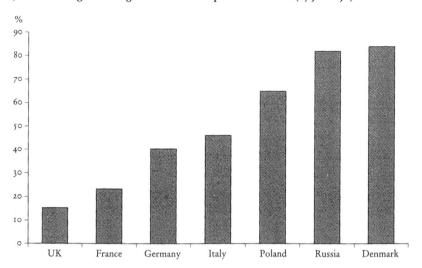

72. Percentage of foreign novels in European literatures (1816, 1850)

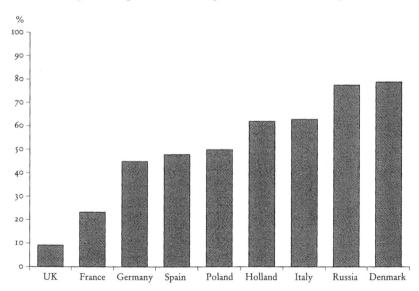

the years around 1750 has become a mere 5 percent by the middle of the following century (figure 73).[10]

These opposite trajectories were intriguing, and I decided to check a few more sources. I found records of earlier British libraries, charted the number of translations, and the drop reappeared, even

[10] But perhaps – it has been objected to these data – translations were unnecessary, since so many people read French, in nineteenth-century Britain. Perhaps. But exactly how many people did so remains unclear, and besides, many people read French in Poland and Italy too, but that didn't keep Polish and Italian publishers from translating a lot of French novels.

---

73. Foreign novels in French and British literature

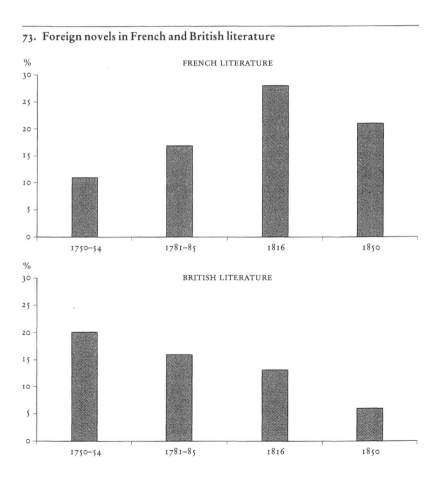

sharper than I had expected (figure 74). Then I went to the Bibliothèque Nationale, which has a wonderful collection of catalogues

---

74. Foreign novels in British circulating libraries (1766–1861)

The (relative) disappearance of foreign novels from the British literary market seems to be concentrated in two distinct phases: the 1790s and the late 1820s. In the first case, British hostility to the French revolution is the most likely explanation (corroborated by the heavy connotations of the villains in figure 10). In the second case, however, the decisive factor is probably the autonomous development of literary production: around 1815–20, British literature comes up with a whole set of narrative forms (historical novels, war stories, nautical tales, silver-fork novels, a revival of oriental tales) that may well have saturated the market, reducing the space for foreign imports.

Catalogues consulted: Lowndes (London 1766), Clay (Warwick 1772), Bell's (London 1778), John Smith (Glasgow 1785), Sanders (Derby 1788?), Lockett (Dorchester 1790), Phorson (Berwick 1790), James Sibbald (Edinburgh 1791?), Sael (London 1793), Yearsley (Bristol 1793), A. Brown (Aberdeen 1795), Mariott (Derby 1795), Angus and Son (Aberdeen 1799), Booth (Norwich 1802), Turner (Beverley 1803?), Rennison & Tarry (South End, Essex 1810), Turner (Beverley 1817), Wilkins (Derby 1817), Ford (Chesterfield 1820?), A. Watson (Aberdeen 1821), Johnson (Beverley 1832), Wyllie and Son (Aberdeen 1833), Jones & Parry (Carnarvon 1835), Ebers' (London 1838), Literary Society (Madras 1839), Lovejoy's (Reading 1845), Columbell's (Derby 1845), Public Library (Beccles 1847), Public Library (Norwich 1847), Davies' (Cheltenham 1849), Henriques' (Cheltenham 1849), Hewitt's (Derby 1849), Kaye's (Newcastle-upon-Tyne 1852), Plowman's (Oxford 1852), Vibert's (Penzance 1855), Athenaeum & Mechanic Institute (Wolverhampton 1856), British Library (London 1861)

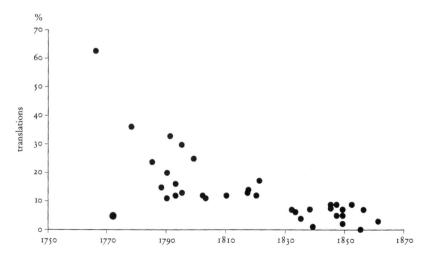

from *cabinets de lecture* (the French equivalent of the circulating library), and looked up comparable data for nineteenth-century *cabinets* of varying location and size (figure 75); and here too the

---

75. Sample of French *cabinets de lecture* (1810–60)

Catalogues consulted: Galignani (Paris 1809), Auzou (Rouen 1811), Houze (Paris 1811), Janet et Cotelle (Paris 1811), Renard (Paris 1811), Garnier (Paris 1818), Goullet (Paris 1821), Hautecoeur (Paris 1822), Mesdames Alexandre (Rouen 1822), Ducrot-Desons (La Cappelle 1823), Gondar-Roblot (Paris 1823), Ridan (Paris 1823), Cassegrain (Havre 1824), Goujon (Paris 1825), Goujon (St-Germain-en-Laye 1825), Mlle Charveys (Saint-Maixent 1825), Malines (St-Jean-Pied-de-Port 1825?), Rosier (Paris 1825), Beauvert Fils (Clermont-Ferrand 1827), Jocquinot (Paris 1828), Galliot (Paris 1831), Janotte (Paris 1832), Jenotte (Saint-Cloud 1832), Alloir (Chevreuse 1833), Cochard (Rocroi 1835?), Lemonnier (Dunkerque 1835?), Leger (St-Omer 1836), Campion (Guines, Boulogne 1838), Fourny-Hairaud (Gueret 1838), Piltan (Paris 1838), Combarel (Dole 1840), François dit Violette (Cherbourg 1840?), Caboche-Lebargy (Roubaix 1841), Jeannot (Paris 1842), Jeannot (St-Hyppolite-sur-le-Doubs 1842), Ober (Douai 1844), Boyer (Chalon-sur-Saône 1845), Dortu (Châlons sur-Marne 1845), Cabinet Central de Lecture (Digione 1847), Arnaud (Havre 1853), Fluteau-Guyot (Chatillons-sur-Seine 1854), Pousset-Remond (Digione 1854), Pujo-Bergedebat (Cauterets 1854), Duverge et Josset (Paris 1855), Duverge et Josset (St-Denis, Ile de la Réunion 1855), Mme Tesselin-Laguerre (Saint-Mihiel 1855), Tumerel-Bertram (St-Omer 1855), Barthes (Castres 1856), Pate Aine (Charleville 1856), Mlle Cattou (Roubaix 1857)

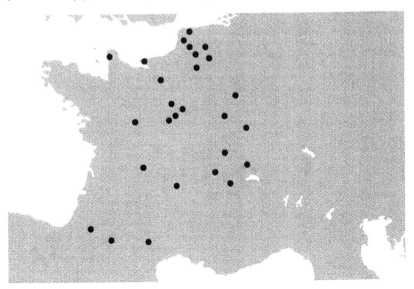

presence of foreign novels – that oscillates for thirty years between 20 and 30 percent, and declines abruptly around 1840, when the generation of Hugo, Dumas, Sue, and Balzac conquers the market – seems largely in agreement with the bibliographical record (figure 76).

'How England became an island', writes Braudel in *The Perspective of the World*; well, this is a similar story: how narrative England becomes an island, repudiating its eighteenth-century familiarity with French books for Victorian autarky.[11] And if we turn from quantitative data to some select qualitative cases, the result is the same. *Eugénie Grandet* and *Old Goriot* are translated 26 years after their original publication; *Elective Affinities*, 45 years; *The Charterhouse of Parma*, 62 years; *The Red and the Black*, 70 years. In the second half of the century, *Madame Bovary* is translated (by Eleanor

---

[11] 'Lists such as [Collyer's in the 1740s] indicate that in the years immediately following *Pamela* the staple works of the circulating libraries were largely translated from the French' (Alan Dugald McKillop, 'English Circulating Libraries, 1725–1750', *The Library*, 1933–4, pp. 484–5). According to James Raven, between 1750 and 1770 'six of the leading twenty and ten of the leading thirty writers were French' (James Raven, *British Fiction 1750–1770*, Delaware University Press, Newark 1987, p. 21).

---

76. Foreign novels in French *cabinets de lecture*

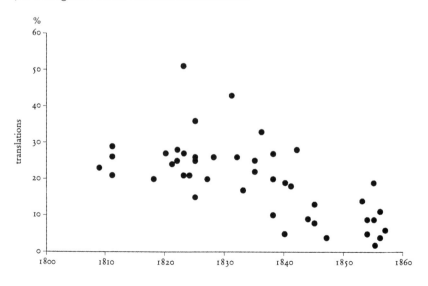

Marx) 29 years after its publication; *Sentimental Education*, 29 years; *Buddenbrooks*, 23 years (and in New York). Some early Russian classics (*Eugene Onegin, Dead Souls, Oblomov, Fathers and Sons*) are translated into French (on average) 20 years after the Russian publication; into English, 43 years after. Or again: in 1869, Mudie's gigantic library in New Oxford Street had *nothing* in English by Voltaire, Diderot, Pushkin, or Balzac (it also didn't have *Werther, Elective Affinities*, and *The Three Musketeers*; at which point I gave up).[12] And a few years later, Henry Vizetelly ends up in jail for translating Zola, while a patriotic attack is launched against the 'open sewers' (*Daily Telegraph*, 1891) of Ibsen's bourgeois dramas.

It seems like the American film market today: expecting nothing from abroad; not curious, not interested. And worse. As *The Novel Newspaper*, a cheap reprint series, put it in one of its ads:

> as regards the French novelists of the days of Victor Hugo, Madame Sand and Paul de Kock, for the total exclusion of [their] works from *The Novel Newspaper* we are proud to acknowledge having received the thanks of the heads of many families . . .[13]

The pride of the censor. There is a *hostility* to foreign forms, here, that recalls the xenophobia behind the French villains and the 'invasion literature' of fictional geography (figures 10 and 66), and that cannot but have had major effects on British narrative as a whole: that must have *impoverished* it – in the sense Virginia Woolf had in mind when she said, and she was right, that *Middlemarch* is one of the few English novels written for adults. Quantity affects form, again, because few foreign novels doesn't simply mean few foreign novels: it means that many great themes and techniques of the age (adultery, politics, Auerbach's 'serious' tone, reality effects, naturalism, novels

---

[12] See Sarah Keith, *Mudie's Select Library: Principal Works of Fiction in Circulation in 1848, 1858, 1869*, Ann Arbor, Michigan 1955. 'Will fashionable fine ladies and gentlemen – wrote Geraldine Jewsbury in one of her reports for Mudie's – read of the painful anxieties of a broken merchant? Will ordinary female readers care to read of the gradations of business speculations?' Which is to say: will they care to read *César Birotteau* or *Lost Illusions*? (Jewsbury is quoted by Guinevere L. Griest, *Mudie's Circulating Library and the Victorian Novel*, Indiana University Press, Bloomington 1970, p. 127).

[13] For *The Novel Newspaper* (1839–42) see Michael Sadleir, *Nineteenth-Century Fiction. A Bibliographical Record*, Cambridge University Press, 1951, vol. II, pp. 142–5.

of ideas . . .) – all of these are almost *denied right of entry into Britain*; while other techniques (fairy-tale structures, happy endings, sentimental moralism, the comic dominant) enjoy as a result a sort of protectionism, thus surviving until the end of the century. And British adults read *David Copperfield*, and it serves them right.[14]

4. A united and uneven market

The DNB. Foreign novels. And then, I decided to look at the presence of cheap reprint series. Figure 77 follows the earliest and most popular of such collections: the initial twenty-four titles of Bentley's Standard Novels, published between 1831 and 1833. As you can see, the graph splits into two broad *plateaux*: large libraries have almost all of the Bentley's novels; small ones, very few. And when I zoomed in on the latter, the scenario was by now a familiar one. Small size had again produced hyper-canonization: the novels of Cooper and Austen, that formed 33 percent of the Bentley's sample, rose here to 75 percent. European novels, for their part, had again disappeared. And then, I noticed something else: three of the five smallest libraries had bought only Bentley's historical novels; a fourth one, only sentimental novels. They had invested in one genre – and given up the rest: no Gothic, no Jacobin novels, no *Frankenstein*, no regional tales . . .

In other words: a small library doesn't choose fewer items from the *entire* morphological spectrum; rather, it reduces *the very extent* of the spectrum. Size affects formal variety – in the sense that it *reduces* variety. Small spaces are not like Noah's ark, with two of

---

[14] The international horizon seems to be even narrower in the case of the working class. In 1875, the Library of the Alliance Cabinet Makers' Association had one French text (by Gustave Aimard) among sixty works of fiction (Stan Shipley, 'The Library of the Alliance Cabinet Makers' Association', *History Workshop*, Spring 1976); thirty years later, when the *Review of Reviews* asked the first large group of Labour MPs to mention the authors that had most influenced them, Mazzini is the only foreign name to appear in the list (see Jonathan Rose, 'How historians study reader response: or, what did Jo think of *Bleak House?*', in John O. Jordan and Robert L. Patten, eds, *Literature in the Marketplace*, Cambridge University Press, 1995, pp. 203–4).

each species; they limit the number of species. 'The number of different species present in a given area', writes Stephen Jay Gould, 'is strongly influenced, if not controlled, by the amount of the habitable area itself'.[15] And so with books: the number of forms is influenced, if not controlled, by the space of the library. Which is to say, by the space of the market. *The Wealth of Nations*, chapter three:

> As it is the power of exchanging that gives occasion to the division of labour, so the extent of this division must always be limited by the extent of that power, or, in other words, by the extent of the market. When the market is very small, no person can have encouragement to dedicate himself entirely to one employment [. . .] There are some sorts of industry, even of the lowest kind, which can be carried on nowhere but in a great town. A porter, for example, can find employment and subsistence in no other place. A village is by much too narrow a space for him; even an ordinary market town is scarce large enough to afford him constant occupation . . .

The extent of the division of labor is limited by the extent of the market . . . This is it. A small library is the sign of a small market: 'too narrow a space', for the increasing division of labor of nineteenth-century narrative; and so, it discourages the more specialized forms (like Jacobin novels, or regional tales, or foreign imports) and selects by contrast the all-purpose, 'generalist' genre of the historical novel.

[15] Stephen Jay Gould, *Ever Since Darwin*, Norton, New York 1977, p. 136.

77. Presence of 'Bentley's Standard Novels' in circulating libraries

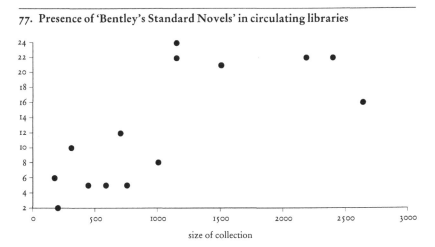

size of collection

And speaking of narrow markets, let me complete this socio-logical sketch with a rapid step backwards: Paul Kaufman's path-breaking article on late eighteenth-century circulating libraries. I have added to Kaufman's data a few catalogues that have surfaced in the intervening years, and the result is in figure 78: in the majority of British towns with a population of 10,000 or fewer, *70, 80, even 90 percent of all available books are novels*. This is not inevitable, in those towns (see the lower part of the graph),[16] but it happens quite frequently – whereas it's unthinkable in London, where novels are at most one-third of the total. And figure 79 is the map of this state of affairs, where the height of the black columns indicates the percent-age of novels in the various locations.

In households with only one book, I said earlier, we find religion; in libraries with only one bookcase, the canon; in towns with only

[16] The small town libraries with fewer novels are John Allen's (Hereford, *ca.* 1790: under 5 percent – but including a 'notable list of children's books' that may affect that figure), Ann Ireland's (Leicester, 1789: 5 percent), and Silver's (Ramsgate, *ca.* 1787: for which Kaufman mentions a 20 percent of fiction, although his own data suggest a figure closer to 35 percent). Once more, the most likely explanation of this difference lies *in the different size* of the libraries: when a collection has 500 volumes or fewer, the percentage of fiction usually jumps well over 70 percent; when it has over 2,000 (as is the case for Allen, Silver, and Ireland), it drops to 30 percent or less. As is to be expected, small libraries are more frequent in small towns, and large libraries in large towns – but the correlation is hardly flawless.

---

78. Percentage of novels in late eighteenth-century circulating libraries

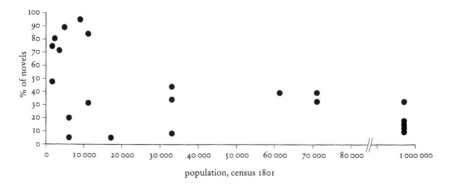

population, census 1801

one library, the novel.[17] This is a map of the novelization of the provinces: the material antecedent for Madame Bovary (who also got her books from a circulating library – and they were all novels). And indeed, in the late nineteenth century, lending statistics and librarians' reports from all over Britain agree that the novel has become the

[17] Same conclusions in Jan Fergus: 'The evidence suggests that small provincial libraries in the late eighteenth century tended to stock mostly fiction' ('Eighteenth-Century Readers in Provincial England', p. 158 n.) A rapid examination of 23 catalogues from small French towns in the first half of the nineteenth century gave even more striking results: most of them stocked only novels, and I have found only two which had less than 85 percent. The same seems to be true of Germany, as described by Reinhard Wittmann: 'Circulating libraries *with a predominantly narrative repertoire* [. . .] were often kept by second-hand dealers, or binders, or persons entirely extraneous to the publishing world; *in smaller towns*, however, several serious and reliable booksellers found themselves forced to align themselves to this commercial trend. In the Duchy of Württenmberg, in 1809, nine circulating libraries out of ten were enterprises [. . .] of this kind, with stocks ranging from 200 to 600 volumes' ('Una rivoluzione della lettura alla fine del XVIII secolo?', in Guglielmo Cavallo and Roger Chartier, eds, *Storia della lettura nel mondo occidentale*, Laterza, Bari–Roma 1995, pp. 364–5; emphasis mine).
   The American data collected by David Kaiser for the period 1765–1866 (*A book for a sixpence. The Circulating Library in America*, Beta Phi Mu, Pittsburgh 1980, Appendixes

79. Percentage of novels in late eighteenth-century circulating libraries

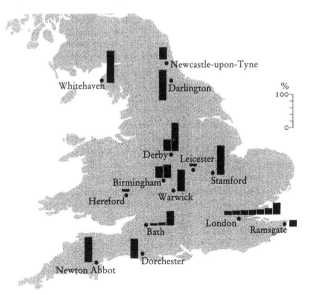

dominant form of provincial reading – if not indeed the *only* form.[18] Novels are not a 'first step' after which (as the Salford Public Library Parliamentary Return for 1856 put it) readers may be 'gradually and progressively drawn from light literature to historical and biographical works'.[19] No, novels are there to stay, 'locking out' by their success most other kinds of reading.[20]

This monopoly of fiction over provincial readers restates this chapter's opening question: a national literature – or an archipelago of local circuits? One system, or many? I don't know about other

I and II) are the only ones that contradict this general trend, with percentages of 'Fiction' and 'Literature' consistently higher in Boston, Baltimore, or New York than in Portsmouth, Newburyport, or Waterville. Usually (though not always) small town libraries with a low percentage of fiction have a high percentage of 'Theology and Religion', suggesting that the displacement of Religion by Fiction that – in Europe – had occurred in the second half of the eighteenth century, was progressing more slowly on American soil.

[18] 'The library Committee [at Stockport] was alarmed to find that fiction constituted 73% of the issues in the first year (1875–76), rising to 80% by the third year' (Thomas Kelly, *A History of Public Libraries in Great Britain 1845–1975*, Library Association, London 1977, p. 51). At Airdrie, 'The library committee would have been delighted if the percentage of fiction issued had gone down, but this it showed no inclination to do', writes W. Craig Strang ('Airdrie Public Library, 1853–1894', *Library Review*, 1985, p. 222). And the Belfast report for 1892–93 indicated 61 percent for prose fiction, plus 18 percent for 'Juvenile Literature' (which was largely composed of fiction) ('Our Readers and What They Read'; read before the Annual Meeting of the Library Association, September 1894).

[19] 'Alas for human hopes', comments Thomas Kelly after quoting the Salford Report: twenty years later, 'in the Return for 1876, it appeared that fiction accounted for 45% of the stock, and 83% of the total lendings' (ibid., p. 51). And discussing other late nineteenth-century returns: 'In a sample of thirteen lending libraries, including all the larger libraries and a selection of the smaller ones, there were only two in which the fiction issues formed less than 50% of total loans. These were Sheffield (30%) and Manchester (48%). In the remainder, it was between 57% at Birmingham and 83% at Bradford and Salford. A similar sample compiled in 1883 shows a range between 55% at Plymouth and 78% at Nottingham: in this list Manchester has risen to 57% and Sheffield to 63%' (p. 77).

The gap between readers' tastes and librarians' wishes was just as wide in workers' libraries: the Social-Democratic Party of Germany's librarians, for instance, wanted to 'lead readers from entertainment material to non-fictional works', but were overcome by a flood of requests for fiction that, between 1908 and 1914, reached 73 percent (Martin Lyons, 'I nuovi lettori nel XIX secolo: donne, fanciulli, operai', in Cavallo and Chartier, eds, *Storia della lettura nel mondo occidentale*, pp. 398–9).

[20] On the 'locking-out' mechanism, see Brian Arthur, 'Competing Technologies, Increasing Returns, and Lock-in by Historical Events', *The Economic Journal*, March 1989, especially pp. 116–17, 126–8.

forms, but for the novel the answer can only be: one. And remember, this was not my initial hypothesis. I expected unevenness; I *wanted* unevenness – circuits moving gradually away from each other, and lending themselves to beautiful maps. And instead, they all converged towards a common literary market: towards the Dictionary of *National* Biography. If anything, the smaller provincial libraries turned out to be more 'national' than the capital itself.[21]

Still: a single mechanism, not a *fair* one. We have seen how unequal the novel's market actually is, with smaller libraries having not just fewer items, but fewer *choices* than larger ones. But the point is that a market with fewer choices offers no alternative to a richer one: if anything, it's more insular, more canonical, more monotonous. More of the same; or perhaps, *less* of the same.

And finally, a unified market – *in England*. Kaufman thirty years ago, and I today, have only worked on English circulating libraries; and since I have so far been unable to find catalogues from mid nineteenth-century Ireland, Scotland, and Wales, I really cannot say whether the unified market extended to the UK as a whole. Some Scottish catalogues of figure 74 (that belong however to a much earlier period), and Simms and M'Intyre's 'Parlour Library' series, which in its initial Belfast years includes nearly 40 percent of translations (five times the English average: a figure that collapses after

---

[21] By 1800, writes John Feather, 'the booksellers had unwittingly pioneered the development of nationwide distribution. The social, political, and cultural influence of this achievement was out of all proportion to its economic scale. Although regional cultures survived, a uniform national culture was superimposed upon them through the uniformity of the printed word' (*Provincial Book Trade in Eighteenth Century England*, Cambridge University Press, 1985, p. 123). The beginning of this 'nationalization of the provinces' is set by Donald Read in the 1760s (*The English Provinces c. 1760–1960. A Study in Influence*, Edward Arnold, London 1964, pp. 18 ff.).

As for France, thus Martin Lyons: 'In the course of the nineteenth century, regional differences disappear a little at a time. The development of literacy slowly eliminates differences in education and [. . .] the several regional audiences are fused together into a single national audience.' And elsewhere, commenting on the 1866 reports of the prefects on rural reading habits: 'The main interest of the questionnaire lies in the fact that the same titles have the same success all over the country. The literary tastes of the Hautes-Pyrénées are not dissimilar, according to the prefects, to those of the Allier, or of the Nord' (Martin Lyons, *Le Triomphe du livre*, Promodis, Paris 1987, pp. 194, 163).

1853, when the 'Parlour Library' moves to London) – these instances suggest that there may indeed be major differences within the British isles. But before making guesses, one needs more data.

5. *Theoretical interlude V. Center and periphery*

'Happy are you in your retirement', wrote Samuel Richardson, from London, to Bishop Hildesley of Sodor and Man, 'where you read what books you choose, either for instruction or entertainment . . .'[22] What books *you* choose? What we have seen so far suggests otherwise. Kenneth Clark:

> The history of European art has been, to a large extent, the history of a series of centres, from each of which radiated a style [. . .] which was metropolitan at its centre, and became more and more provincial as it reached the periphery. [. . .] It may be said that provincialism is merely a matter of distance from a centre, where standards of skill are higher and patrons more exacting.[23]

I don't know about European art, but the history of the novel certainly supports Clark's thesis. Bakhtin's belief in the '*decentralizing forces*' of novelistic writing – already dubious for fictional geography, as the previous chapters have shown – clashes here with a

---

[22] The episode is mentioned by Roy McKeen Wiles, 'The Relish for Reading in Provincial England Two Centuries Ago', in Paul J. Korshin, ed., *The Widening Circle. Essays on the Circulation of Literature in Eighteenth-Century Europe*, Pennsylvania University Press, 1976, p. 87.

[23] Kenneth Clark, *Provincialism*, The English Association Presidential Address, 1962, p. 3. Clark's text reproduces almost word by word an older statement by Giorgio Pasquali: 'successful innovations radiate most often from the center towards the periphery, and they don't necessarily always reach it' (*Storia della tradizione e critica del testo*, Le Monnier, Firenze 1934, p. 7). More recently, thus William McNeill: 'Diffusion of skill and knowledge from one community to its neighbors and neighbors' neighbors constitutes the central process of human history [. . .] With the rise of civilizations, high skills concentrated in a few metropolitan centers' ('Diffusion in History', in Peter J. Hugill and D. Bruce Dickson, *The Transfer and Transformation of Ideas and Material Culture*, Texas A&M University Press, 1988, pp. 75–6).

The most explicit and spirited attempt to falsify Clark's thesis (Enrico Castelnuovo and Carlo Ginzburg, 'Centro e periferia', in *Storia dell'arte italiana*, vol. I, Einaudi, Torino 1979, pp. 283–352), actually ends up strengthening it, as Castelnuovo and Ginzburg fail to find a *single* long-term innovation originating outside the few centers of Italian painting.

geography of publishing where the center holds an almost unchallenged sway. Be it mid eighteenth-century Britain (figure 80), or mid nineteenth-century Italy (figure 81), the message is the same: the novel is *the most centralized of all literary genres*. And its centralization increases with the passage of time: when the curate and the barber decide to purge Don Quixote's library of all chivalric romances, they find seventeen such texts, distributed rather evenly across nine different cities; two hundred years later, they would have discovered that Madrid publishes as many foreign novels as the rest

80. Publication sites of British novels 1750–70

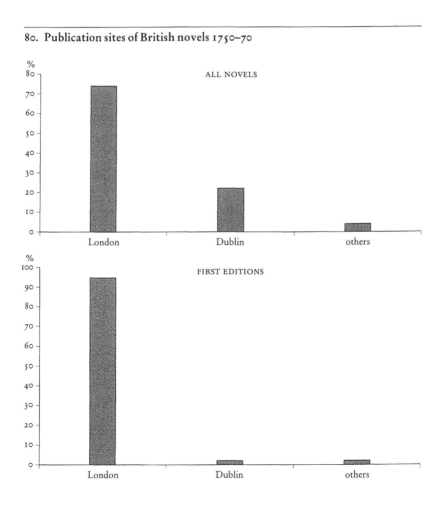

%
80
ALL NOVELS
70
60
50
40
30
20
10
0

London   Dublin   others

%
100
FIRST EDITIONS
90
80
70
60
50
40
30
20
10
0

London   Dublin   others

of Spain put together (and with Barcelona, almost 90 percent: figures 82 and 83).

From provincialism – to centralization. Paradoxical? Not really, they are the two sides of the same coin, because provincialism is not so much a matter of difference from the center, but of *enforced similarity*: the conviction that 'real' life is only to be experienced in Paris (or London, or Moscow) – while life in the provinces is merely a shadow. And the novels that arrive from the center, with provincial malaise as one of their favorite themes, reinforce the circle of dependence over and over again.[24]

[24] The provinces lend themselves particularly well to novels of adultery – *Madame Bovary, La Regenta, Effi Briest, The Illustrious House of Ramires, The Viceroys* . . . – where the opposition of husband and lover becomes an allegory of the contrast between provincial boredom and the slightly corrupt charm of the capital.

81. Publication sites of three literary forms in mid nineteenth-century Italy

From 1843 to 1845, 20 novels are published in Tuscany: all of them in Florence. By contrast, 20 plays and 34 poetry collections are published in twelve other Tuscan towns. The same results emerge from a sample taken in Lombardy: of 98 novels, 97 are published in Milan (the other one in Bergamo), whereas 86 plays and 51 poetry collections are published in seven other Lombard towns.

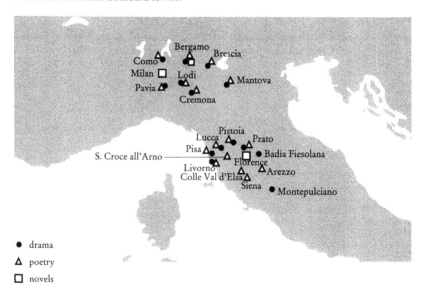

● drama
▲ poetry
□ novels

82. Publication sites of chivalric romances in Don Quixote's library

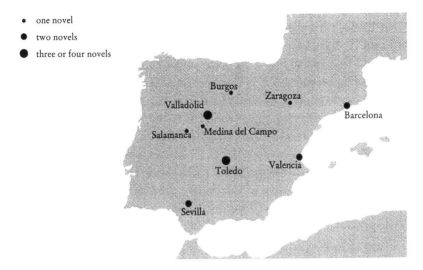

- one novel
- two novels
- three or four novels

Burgos
Zaragoza
Valladolid
Barcelona
Salamanca   Medina del Campo
Toledo   Valencia
Sevilla

83. Publication sites of foreign novels in Spain, first half of the nineteenth century

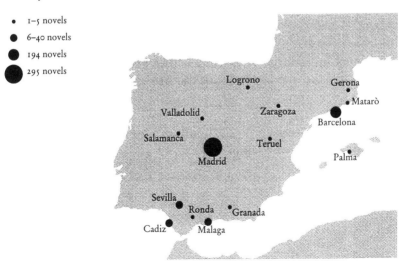

- 1–5 novels
- 6–40 novels
- 194 novels
- 295 novels

Logrono
Gerona
Mataró
Valladolid   Zaragoza
Barcelona
Salamanca   Teruel
Palma
Madrid
Sevilla
Ronda   Granada
Cadiz   Malaga

Centralization, enforced similarity, dependence . . . This was not a painless process. 'In the relation between center and periphery', write Castelnuovo and Ginzburg, 'we don't encounter diffusion, but conflict'.[25] Kenneth Clark mentions for his part 'the formidable power of the central tradition – formidable and destructive',[26] while Torsten Hägerstrand, the great theorist of spatial diffusion, focuses on 'the shadow-side' of successful innovations, with their 'unintended, and frequently deplorable, consequences'.[27]

Not diffusion but conflict, then. Or, better, diffusion *as* conflict: between the novels that come from the center, and the cultural forms that are most typical of provincial publishing; first of all, devotional literature. In the century of the novel's take-off, write Julien Brancolini and Marie-Thérèse Bouyssy, 'religious works [. . .] remain the basic product, the "classic" of the provinces'. And then:

> Judging from provincial print runs, 'the supernatural foundation of the social order' mentioned by François Furet for the years 1723–1727 remains surprisingly unchanged throughout the eighteenth century [. . .] The provincial *milieu* appears characterized by a permanence of religious curiosity.[28]

Whenever a cultural novelty starts spreading its influence, writes A.L. Kroeber, it always encounters some kind of 'resistance', due to 'the presence in the recipient cultures of material and systems which are, or are felt to be, irreconcilable with the invading traits or system'.[29] And this is probably what happened to the novel's 'invading system' when it first reached the provinces, and clashed with devotional literature. But resistance was weak, and rapidly overcome. After the 'novelization' of the British provinces in the late

[25] Castelnuovo and Ginzburg, 'Centro e periferia', p. 286.

[26] Kenneth Clark, *Provincialism*, p. 5.

[27] Torsten Hägerstrand, 'Some Unexplored Problems in the Modeling of Culture Transfer and Transformation', in Hughill and Dickson, *The Transfer and Transformation of Ideas and Material Culture*, p. 231.

[28] Julien Brancolini and Marie-Thérèse Bouyssy, 'La vie provinciale du livre à la fin de l'Ancien Régime', in *Livre et société dans la France du XVIIIe siècle*, vol. II, Mouton, Paris–The Hague 1970, pp. 11–13.

[29] A.L. Kroeber, 'Diffusionism', in Amitai Etzioni and Eva Etzioni, eds, *Social Change*, Basic Books, New York 1964, p. 143.

eighteenth century, here is Robert Darnton on the wider European scenario:

> The rise of the novel had balanced a decline in religious literature, and in almost every case the turning point could be located in the second half of the 18th century, especially in the 1770s, the years of the *Wertherfieber* [...] The last sentences of *Werther* seemed to announce the advent of a new reading public along with the death of traditional Christian culture: 'Workmen carried [the body]. No priest accompanied it.'[30]

A new reading public. Which chooses metropolitan novels over provincial devotion; and which also chooses *long narratives over shorter ones*. Musing on the fuzzy borders between the novel and other forms, James Raven mentions the 'often more problematic provincial work', probably struck by how *short* provincial 'novels' can be.[31] In eighteenth-century France, writes Geneviève Bollème of Rouen's *Bibliothèque Bleue* – which was the greatest publishing venture of the European provinces – there is a 'harsh competition' between '*les grands romans*' and another form 'that one may well call "*les petits romans*" (between 24 and 48 pages)';[32] in the first half of the nineteenth century, Martin Lyons finds the same geographical pattern, with provincial publishers specializing in collections of tales

---

[30] Robert Darnton, *The Kiss of Lamourette*, Norton, New York 1990, p. 161. As Darnton points out, virtually all book historians agree that the publication of fiction developed, throughout Western Europe, at the expense of devotion. This said, one major question must still be answered: did the novel replace devotional literature because it was a *fundamentally secular form* – or because it was *religion under a new guise*? If the former, we have a genuine opposition, and the novel opens a truly new phase in European culture; if the latter, we have a case of historical transformism, where the novel supports the long duration of symbolic conventions. Here, clearly enough, quantitative methods are no longer useful: they can establish the relative strength of devotional and fictional publishing – but cannot say whether fiction *resembles* devotion, and how. This is a task for morphological analysis, and the literary history of the future.

[31] Raven, *British Fiction 1750–1770*, p. 5. The six original 'novels' published in the English provinces between 1750 and 1770 (in Liverpool, Birmingham, York, and Wolverhampton) are 70, 117, 60, 352, 205, and 40 pages long.

[32] Geneviève Bollème, 'Littérature populaire et littérature de colportage au 18e siècle', in *Livre et société dans la France du XVIIIe siècle*, vol. I, Mouton, Paris–The Hague 1965, p. 86.

rather than novels and other long works.[33] And a radical *reduction*, at all levels, had indeed been the secret of the *Bibliothèque Bleue*: shorter books, shorter chapters, shorter pages, shorter paragraphs, shorter sentences...

The long against the short. Which is to say, written culture (that can easily afford the large format) against oral culture (more often constrained to the short). 'The triumph of the book', writes Martin Lyons,

> superseded a popular and oral literature which contained the ingredients, in Gramscian terms, of an alternative world-view, however unsystematically and inarticulately this was expressed. Novels entered the sack of the colporteur alongside the almanacs, and the railway and local bookshop made the colporteur himself redundant. Popular literary culture could not long survive the industrialization of book production, the nationalization of the book market, and growing conformity in literary consumption.[34]

The industrialization of book production... The late eighteenth century saw an 'early industrial revolution in entertainment', writes Peter Burke, in the course of which, 'as elsewhere in the 18th century economy, large-scale enterprises were driving out small ones':[35] and larger cities, where capital for large-scale enterprises (and long bulky books) was easier to find, gained an irreversible advantage. While the consumption of fiction was becoming more and more *widespread*, then, its production was becoming more and more *centralized*, both within each individual nation-state, and within the larger system of European states. It's the same geographical polarization that will

---

[33] Of all editions of Perrault's *Contes*, 53.9 percent were published in the provinces; of Florian's *Fables*, 47.1 percent; of La Fontaine's *Fables*, 45.9 percent; of Defoe's *Robinson Crusoe*, 38.3 percent; of Tasso's *Jerusalem Delivered*, 33.3 percent; of Saint-Pierre's *Paul et Virginie*, 28.1 percent; of Racine's *Théâtre*, 15.6 percent. *Télémaque*, with 54 percent provincial editions, is the only exception (Lyons, *Le Triomphe du livre*, p. 103).

An even more unbalanced pattern emerges from the Italian samples of 1843–45 (figure 81), where provincial towns publish a dozen short narratives (or collections of tales) – and only one novel.

[34] Martin Lyons, 'Towards a National Literary Culture in France: Homogeneity and the 19th Century Reading Public', *History of European Ideas*, vol. 16, nos. 1–3, 1993, p. 250.

[35] Peter Burke, *Popular Culture in Early Modern Europe*, Harper & Row, New York 1978, p. 249.

implacably return with each successive form of mass entertainment –
film, radio, TV. So, let us take a closer look.

II

> In place of the old wants, satisfied by the productions of
> the country, we find new wants, requiring for their satis-
> faction the products of distant lands and climes. In place
> of the old local seclusion and self-sufficiency, we have
> intercourse in every direction, universal inter-dependence
> of nations. And as in material, so also in intellectual pro-
> duction. The intellectual creations of individual nations
> become common property. National one-sidedness and
> narrow-mindedness become more and more impossible,
> and from the numerous national and local literatures there
> arises a world literature.
>
> KARL MARX AND FRIEDRICH ENGELS,
> *Manifesto of the Communist Party*

6. *The three Europes*

The novel in Europe, and its first international bestseller: *Don
Quixote*. If one looks at publishing records, Cervantes' success
resembles the classic stone thrown in a pond: it sends out from the
Spanish peninsula a series of waves – translation-waves, as it were
(figures 84a–c). The first wave occurs right away, within one to two
generations, along a western diagonal running from London to
Venice (through Holland, France, and the German territories): a
very precocious international market, already synchronized in the
early seventeenth century. It's a striking beginning (in the mid nineteenth century, it will take *Old Goriot* almost thirty years to travel
from Paris to London!); but then, for over a century, nothing. One is
reminded of a chapter in Braudel's *Mediterranean*: 'space, enemy
number one'. In France and Britain, editions of Cervantes multiply,
but new translations must wait for the end of the eighteenth century:
Denmark, Russia, Poland, Portugal, Sweden (and the affinity, again,
between the novel and the nation-state). Then a third wave, in the

84a–c. *Don Quixote*, European translations

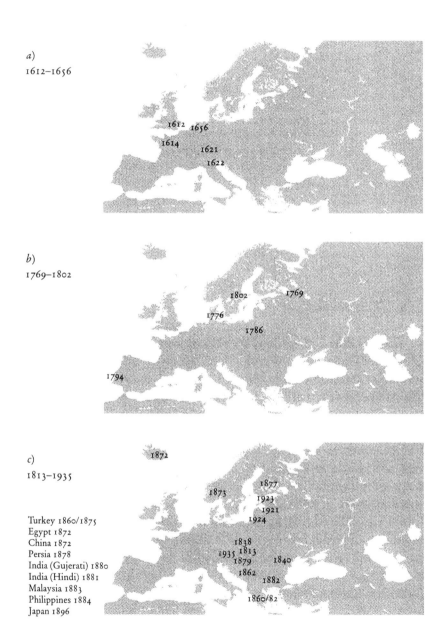

a)
1612–1656

b)
1769–1802

c)
1813–1935

Turkey 1860/1875
Egypt 1872
China 1872
Persia 1878
India (Gujerati) 1880
India (Hindi) 1881
Malaysia 1883
Philippines 1884
Japan 1896

Habsburg and Ottoman empires, the Mitteleuropa (including a Yiddish version in 1848), the northern rim; and also, in the last thirty years of the century, in a large group of Asian countries. And the diffusion continues well into the twentieth century, in linguistic areas that become progressively smaller.

'Space is the face of a gigantic clock', says Hägerstrand of the diffusion of technology (and literary forms *are* technologies of a kind): space is a gigantic clock, and the things that move across it are its hands.[36] True. Like these three or four waves, that show the non-contemporaneity of Europe: the different 'literary epochs' inhabited by its various cultural spaces. Exactly *how many* there are of these spaces is, of course, far from obvious, because the spatio-temporal continuum can be sliced in more than one way: one may take individual nations as the unit of analysis, for instance, and then Europe is *de facto* divided into twenty or thirty cultures. Or one may focus on Curtius' 'Romania', and European literature becomes one, indivisible. Or finally, one may follow the logic of 'world-system' theory, and identify as the significant analytical unit neither the continent as a whole nor the single nation, but three main positions within the European system: three Europes, as it were. At one extreme, what Wallerstein calls the 'core': a precocious, versatile, and very small group (like the seventeenth-century diagonal of figure 84a). At the opposite extreme, the 'periphery': a very large group, but with very little freedom, and little creativity. And in between these two positions, a hybrid cluster combining features of both: the 'semiperiphery'. An area of transition, of combined development: of decline out of the core (as for Spain, or Italy); or conversely (as for the Russian novel of the nineteenth century), of ascent from the periphery into the core.

The three Europes had already emerged in the Columbia study of 1992 that I mentioned earlier. While trying to quantify the 'rise of the

---

[36] 'Some Unexplored Problems', p. 217. Hägerstrand is quoting Friedrich Ratzel's *Anthropogeographie* (Stuttgart 1912, p. 411), which in the early part of the century stimulated several lines of geographical inquiry.

European novel', for instance, we quickly realized that there was not *one*, but (at least) three such take-offs: the first around 1720–1750 (in the core: France, Britain, and a little later Germany); the second around 1820–1850 (for a half dozen countries or so); and a third one, later still, for all the others. And the same pattern emerged from translation routes: at one extreme, a small group of countries (two or three: France, Britain, and Germany; France, Britain, and Russia) – a very small group that exported intensely in every direction; at the other extreme, a very large group that *imported* a lot, and exported almost nothing. And in between, 'regional' powers, as in the *Buddenbrooks* of figure 85: a widespread, immediate success in northeastern, Hanseatic Europe; but until the Nobel in 1929 not a single translation west of the Rhine, or south of the Danube.

Two, three Europes. With France and Britain always in the core; most other countries always in the periphery; and in between a variable group, that changes from case to case. But can we be more precise, and actually *measure* the difference between these three positions? To this decisive (and difficult) question I can only offer a limited answer. Limited, because I consider only eight or nine countries; and confine myself to translations (which are only one side of the question); and work with national bibliographies (that differ widely in their reliability). And then, so many variables are here simultaneously at play, that it's difficult to do them all justice.

7. *A bibliographical investigation*

To measure the internal variation of the European system, I constructed a sample of popular British novels,[37] and followed their

---

[37] The sample consisted of 104 novels, divided in fifteen sets: nine sentimental novels from 1800 to 1815; six novels by Scott (three early ones, three late ones); five 'oriental tales', five 'nautical tales', five war stories (popular genres of the 1820s and 1830s); twelve silver-fork novels; eight local/regional narratives; five each of Bulwer-Lytton's, Ainsworth's, and G.P.R. James' historical best-sellers; seven novels by Dickens (two early ones; two Christmas stories; three late ones); seven mid-century religious novels; ten sentimental novels from around 1850; eight industrial novels; and eight sensation novels.

85*a–b.* *Buddenbrooks*, European translations

a)
1903–29

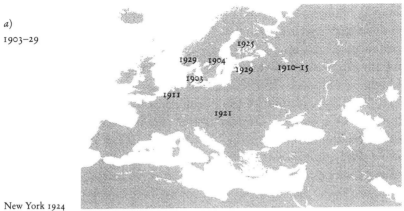

New York 1924

b)
1930–86

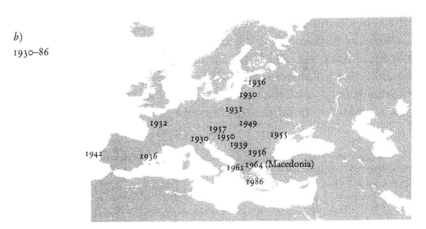

Tel Aviv 1930
Japan 1932
Turkey 1955
Egypt 1961
China 1962
India 1978

fortunes in a group of nations which had reasonably good bibliographies, and from which I expected rather different results: Denmark, France, Hungary, Italy, and Poland. I checked how many of the texts in the sample had been translated, how often, and how quickly. Once certain patterns began to emerge, I double-checked them by extending the sample in both directions: with the help of Margaret Cohen, I constructed a sample of French novels, comparable to the British one,[38] and then broadened the European scenario, by adding to the initial five countries Great Britain, the Netherlands, Rumania (whose national bibliography unfortunately stops, like Mr Ramsay in *To the Lighthouse*, at the letter 'R'), and Spain (whose best repertoire poses a similar problem, because it stops in 1850).[39] The maps of figure 86*a–v* visualize the results of my investigation.

Let us begin at one extreme of the spectrum, with the great successes of the nineteenth century: Scott, Bulwer-Lytton, most of Dickens, and sensation novels from the British sample; sentimental novels, Dumas, Sue, and Hugo from the French one (figure 86*abcd-pqrs*). It is a regular, even monotonous pattern: all of Europe reading the same books, with the same enthusiasm, and roughly in the same years (when not months). All of Europe unified by a desire, not for

[38] The French sample consisted of 48 novels, divided in seven sets: thirteen sentimental novels from 1795 to 1810; eight minor historical novels from the 1820s; seven early realist texts, by Balzac and Stendhal; four novels by Hugo; five 'romans champêtres' by George Sand; seven novels by Sue; and four by Dumas.

[39] I have consulted the following bibliographical repertoires. For Britain: *Nineteenth Century Short Title Catalogue*, Series I (1801–1816) and Series II (1816–1870); *British Library Catalogue*.

For Denmark: Erland Munch-Petersen, *A Bibliography of Translations into Danish 1800–1900 of Prose Fiction from Germanic and Romance Languages*, København 1976.

For France: *Bibliographie de la France*, Paris 1811–56; Otto Lorenz, *Catalogue général de la librairie française, 1840–1865, 1866–1875, 1876–1885, 1886–1890* (Paris 1868, 1876, 1887, 1924); M.G. Devonshire, *The English Novel in France 1830–1870*, University of London Press 1929.

For Hungary: Kertbeny, *Ungarns Deutsche Bibliographie*; *Magyarország Bibliographíaja 1712–1860*, Budapest 1890; *Magyar Könyvészet, 1860–75, 1886–1900, 1901–1910*, Budapest 1890–1917.

For Italy: *CLIO, Catalogo dei libri italiani dell'Ottocento (1801–1900)*, Editrice Bibliografica, Milano 1991.

'realism' (the mediocre fortune of Stendhal and Balzac leaves no doubts on this point) – not for realism, but for what Peter Brooks has called 'the melodramatic imagination': a rhetoric of stark contrasts that is present a bit everywhere, and is perfected by Dumas and Sue (and Verdi), who are the most popular writers of the age.

This common narrative market, however, contracts rapidly as one looks down the columns of figure 86. First Rumania; then Poland and Hungary; then Italy and Spain: the eastern, then the southern part of the continent disappear from the chart; they import fewer and fewer instances of each given form, and end up 'losing' this or that form altogether. Lack of interest? More probably, *lack of space.* Rumania imports far fewer forms than Italy, or Denmark, because it is a much smaller market: and a smaller market, as we have seen with circulating libraries, does not behave like a large one, on a smaller scale: it behaves *differently*. Instead of importing one-third, or one-tenth, of every available form, it selects very few of them, and 'locks out' the rest. Tons of Dumas', Hugo's, Bulwer-Lytton's melodramas, then: but no Captain Marryat, no *Our Village*, no oriental tales, no industrial or silver-fork novels . . .

There are only so many novels that the Rumanian or the Spanish market can absorb every year: once the limit is reached, the gates close. But close *how*? Why are some forms accepted, and others rejected? First of all, because of sheer *saturation*, as in maps 86*efv*. Ainsworth, James, the countless French historical novels: European markets have been so flooded by this form that a certain amount of

For the Netherlands: *Alphabetische Naamlijst van Boeken, 1790–1832*, Amsterdam 1835; *Alphabetische Naamlijst van Boeken, Plaat-en Kaartwerken, 1833–1849*, Amsterdam 1858; *Brinkman's Catalogus der Boeken, Plaat-en Kaartenwerken, 1850–1882*, Amsterdam 1884.

For Poland: Karol Estreicher, *Bibliografia Polska*, Krakow 1881–1939.

For Rumania: Ioan Bianu, Nerva Hodos, Dan Simonescu, *Bibliografia Romaneasca Vecha*, Bucuresti 1912–36; Gabriel Strempel, *Bibliografia Romaneasca Moderna 1831–1918*, Bucuresti 1984–89 (this repertoire stops at the letter 'R').

For Spain: José Fernandez Montesinos, *Introducción a una historia de la novela en España en el siglo XIX; seguida del Esbozo de una bibliografía española de traducciones de novelas (1800–1850)*, Madrid 1966.

86a–o. European diffusion of British novels

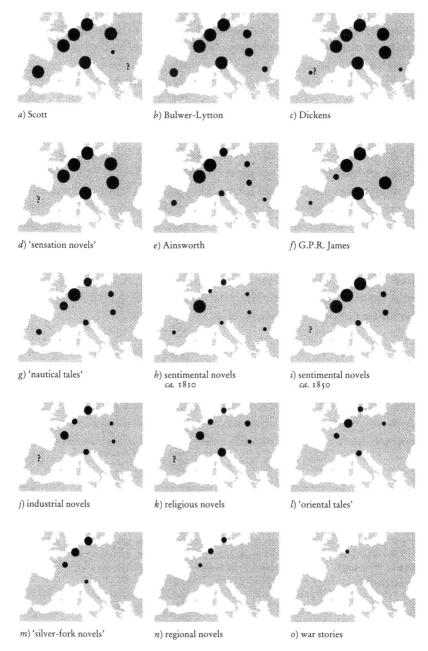

a) Scott

b) Bulwer-Lytton

c) Dickens

d) 'sensation novels'

e) Ainsworth

f) G.P.R. James

g) 'nautical tales'

h) sentimental novels
    ca. 1810

i) sentimental novels
    ca. 1850

j) industrial novels

k) religious novels

l) 'oriental tales'

m) 'silver-fork novels'

n) regional novels

o) war stories

86*p–v.* European diffusion of French novels

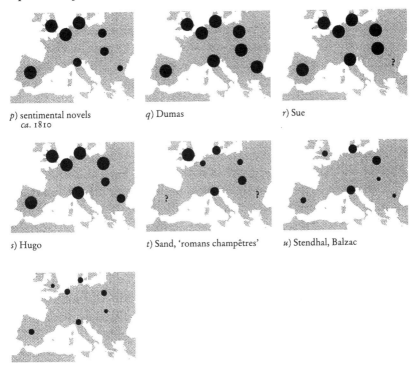

p) sentimental novels
    ca. 1810

q) Dumas

r) Sue

s) Hugo

t) Sand, 'romans champêtres'

u) Stendhal, Balzac

v) minor historical novels

● sample entirely translated

● the majority of the texts in the sample
   has been translated

● about half of the texts in the sample
   have been translated

• one or two sporadic translations

? bibliographic data irretrievable or insufficient

resistance has become almost inevitable. So, France and Poland still translate many novels by Ainsworth, but few or none by James; Italy and Hungary, exactly the reverse: a lot of James, and very little Ainsworth. Are there specific reasons for these opposite choices? I doubt it, Ainsworth and James write very much the same kind of novel; but there is less room for historical novels *in general*, and one of them, for whatever contingent reason, loses ground.

After saturation, *selection* in the proper sense: the choice between different competing forms. In maps 86*g*–*o*, for instance, the Italian market is clearly contracting – but is still very open (unlike most of Europe) to the religious novels of map 86*k*. Or look at the diffusion of British sentimental novels in maps 86*hi*: always high in northern Europe, and low in the East and the South. In all these cases, the geographical pattern suggests *a cultural affinity between the specific form and the specific market*: between Catholic Italy, I mean, and *Fabiola (or, The Church of the Catacombs)*, written by Cardinal Wiseman, and translated three times in a year (in Milan, Turin, and Naples). Or between the 'affective individualism' of British sentimental novels, and the wealthy European North-West, where this value is certainly much more widespread than elsewhere.

If the size of the market makes selection inevitable, then (after all, no market is large enough for *all* nineteenth-century novels!), its *direction* is determined by specific cultural forces. It is Catholicism that 'selects' religious novels for the Italian audiences, just as a greater emancipation of women selects narratives of free emotional choice in Protestant countries. And alongside this 'positive' selection, the 'negative' one of figure 86*mno* is also at work: the slaughter of novels that had all been very popular in Britain – but barely survive (if at all) in the large northern markets, and nowhere else. And from these most unlucky of forms a common denominator seems to emerge: Britishness. Upper class slang in silver-fork novels, narrow local traditions in regional narratives, and plain nationalism, in war stories: all traits that may well have delighted British readers – but must have bored and annoyed all the others.

So far, I have looked at the maps from the viewpoint of forms: historical novels are successful across Europe, sentimental ones in the North, religious novels in Catholic countries, war stories nowhere at all . . . But we can also switch our perspective, and assume the viewpoint of the different countries, trying to establish the extent of their narrative imports. The two matrixes of figure 87, elaborated on Serge Bonin's advice, may offer the beginning of an answer. If one reads them from left to right, they reveal a first group of countries that have access to (almost) all the novels in the sample: Denmark, Spain, and Britain for French novels; Holland, Denmark, and France for British ones. And from this first group the matrix slides gradually all the way to the opposite pole (Rumania; and possibly Spain for British novels), where by contrast only a small minority of forms is successfully imported. Where one should draw the line separating one group from the next is of course far from obvious (especially in the French matrix): it is an interpretive decision – on which Bonin, for instance, had a different view, and suggested 'slicing' the data otherwise. But whatever the choice, the *internal differentiation* of the system seems a well-established fact: especially in the British matrix, which is much richer in data.

A divided Europe. But divided really in *three* groups, as I have claimed earlier on? This depends on what one 'sees' – quite literally – in the matrixes of figure 87, as well as in the diagrams of figure 88 (that show the percentages of successful imports in the different countries). For my part, I see this. Three countries that seem to be *always* in the leading group: France, Britain, Denmark: the center, the core of the system.[40] Then, two or three countries with a very uneven behavior: Spain (many French novels, and very few British ones), Holland (the reverse), and partly Italy. Then again, two countries (Poland and Hungary) that are limited to a half-dozen forms, or

---

[40] Mind you, the core of the system as far as translations are concerned. A different variable (precocity of the novel's take-off, output and variety of the national literature, exports, etc.) would probably produce a different outcome, with Denmark being replaced by Spain, or Germany, or Russia. Eventually, from the intersection of all these partial subsystems, we could construct a detailed image of the 'European novelistic system' as a whole. Unfortunately, this result is still nowhere in sight.

87. Diffusion of French and British novels in nineteenth-century Europe

The matrix simultaneously visualizes the 'hold' of a specific form in the various European countries, and the internal variety of the individual national markets. The homogeneity of the European cultural system is greatest in the top left sector of the matrixes, and decreases as one moves to the right and the bottom.

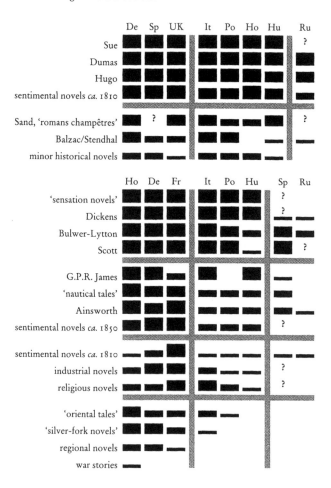

 sample entirely translated

■ the large majority of texts included in the sample has been translated

■ about half of the texts in the sample have been translated

— one or two sporadic translations

? bibliographic data irretrievable or insufficient

88. Diffusion percentages of French and British novels

The diagrams visualize the importation of the individual novels (vertical axis), and sets (horizontal axis) included in the two samples. The internal divisions of the European system emerge quite clearly from the conjunction of the two data.

N.B. In these diagrams, and in those of the following figure, a set is considered 'successfully imported' only if all its texts (or equivalent ones) are translated by the end of the nineteenth century. The figure makes use of percentages because some bibliographies are incomplete, and simple numerical results would therefore be extremely misleading. Unfortunately, this does not mean that the use of percentages is above suspicion; even leaving aside the differences in the bibliographical sources, the British sample includes a larger number of 'weak' forms than does the French sample (a fact to be kept in mind in the course of the discussion that follows).

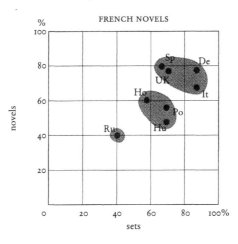

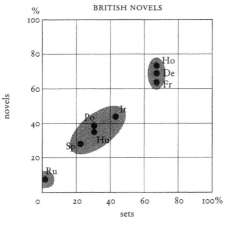

little more. And finally, isolated, Rumania (that may however be plausibly joined, in the case of British novels, by Spain, Hungary, and Poland).

So: a small group with easy access to a lot of European narrative; two groups in the middle, that in their different ways have access to 30–50 percent of the market; and a country at the bottom, with just about one form per generation. There is only *one* country (in that 'peripheral' position where one would expect many more) for this reason, presumably: because at the periphery of Europe the bibliographical tools that I have used either don't exist, or have remained inaccessible to me. Almost by definition, *the periphery of a system is the place where data are least abundant*: this is why it is here 'represented' by Rumania alone. But the contraction of the market that emerges from these matrixes seems too pronounced and steady a trend not to have affected all other European countries.

Three Europes – probably. And then, in all three, a long and bitter rivalry between the continent's two narrative superpowers. Look at how Spain and Holland switch places in figures 87 and 88: Spain with its passion for French novels, but not British ones – and Holland the other way around. It is the sign of a struggle between the two core literatures, that divides the European system in zones of symbolic influence: a struggle for cultural hegemony, in which France seems to have clearly prevailed (figure 89). It is as if the Hundred Years War won by Britain in 1815 had repeated and reversed itself on the cultural front, making of Paris, as it were, the Hollywood of the nineteenth century. In southern and eastern Europe, French novels vastly outnumber British ones (in Italy, at mid century, the ratio is around eight to one), while even in the Protestant North the two rivals are more or less even (in Denmark, Dumas is the most reprinted author of the century). And French superiority emerges clearly in the case of comparable genres: Sand's countryside novels, for instance, that are so much more successful than their British equivalents; or French sentimental novels at the turn of the century, that are translated *en masse* a bit everywhere – whereas their British counterparts remain confined to the North.

I am not sure how to explain this supremacy of the French novel. It may be the recoil and *contrappasso* of Britain's growing insularity, that loses touch (relatively speaking) with continental tastes. Then again, French is the language of educated Europe, and French novels can thus travel faster and farther, occupying cultural niches before their rivals. And finally, the asymmetry may be the result of major morphological differences between the two traditions. But if the explanation is still unclear, the fact itself seems to me unmistakable; and not by chance, when American films and television invaded the European market (exactly like Dumas and *confrères* a century ago), French culture launched a sort of crusade against them. Wonderful thing, symbolic hegemony; and no one gives it up without a struggle.

8. *'A universal inter-dependence of nations'*

So, the European novel has a core in France and Britain. Well . . . we knew that. We knew that; but perhaps, as the *Phenomenology of Mind* put it, 'the well-known in general, being *well*-known, is actually *not* known': it is so familiar, so obvious, that one no longer really sees it, and its implications remain unexplored. Beginning with the

---

89. Uneven success of French and British novels in nineteenth-century Europe

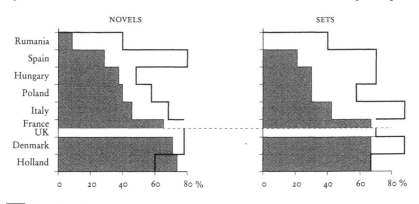

 French novels

British novels

fact that, in the history of European literature, the existence of such a narrow core is completely unusual. The Europe of ballads, for instance, has no center: folklorists describe it as a sort of chessboard, where forms arise locally, and *remain* local: confined to 'small, stable, self-sufficient communities', writes William Entwhistle.[41] Or again: for Peter Burke, the Europe of late oral epics is a system of borders: no center, again, but two or three great symbolic divides, like the one between Christianity and Islam.[42] Another border, in the shape of a crescent, is for Dominique Fernandez the space of the Baroque (figure 90). In other cases, the geography of a form transcends the limits of Europe altogether: short narratives, for instance, arise not really in a 'European', but rather in a 'Mediterranean' network, with a powerful Indian and Arabic component (still visible in the Eastern setting of so many European short stories, as in figures 23 and 24 in the first chapter).[43] Or look at Carlo Ginzburg's map of *Cinderella* in *Ecstasies* (figure 91): for a specific variant of the plot, Brittany is separated from France, and Sardinia from Italy – and morphologically linked to south-east Asia, or the Bay of Bengal.

Different forms, different Europes. Each genre has its geography – its geometry, almost: *but they are all figures without a center.* See here how strange novelistic geography is – and doubly strange. Because, first, the novel closes European literature to all external influences: it strengthens, and perhaps it even establishes its *Europeanness*. But then this most European of forms proceeds to deprive most of Europe of all creative autonomy: two cities, London and Paris, rule the entire continent for over a century, publishing half (if not more) of all European novels. It's a ruthless, unprecedented *centralization* of European literature. Centralization: the center, the

---

[41] William Entwhistle, *European Balladry*, Clarendon, Oxford 1939, p. 7.

[42] Burke, *Popular Culture*, pp. 57, 255.

[43] 'Theodor Benfey, in his *Panchatantra* [. . .] showed how, during the Middle Ages, this old collection of fables was translated from Sanskrit, with Pehlevi, Arabic, and Hebrew as intermediate links, into Latin, and from Latin into later, vulgar tongues' (Carl von Sydow, 'Geography and Folk-Tale Oicotypes', in *Selected Papers on Folklore*, Rosenkilde and Bagger, Copenhagen 1948, p. 45). See also Peter Burke, *Popular Culture*, p. 55: 'Indeed, it would be a mistake to stop at the edge of Europe [. . .] Arab folktales like those in *The Book of Sindbad* and Indian folktales (like those in the *Panchatantra*) were circulating in Europe long before 1500.'

well-known fact; but seen for what it really is: not a given but a process. And a very *unlikely* process: the exception, not the rule of European literature.

With the novel, then, *a common literary market* arises in Europe. One market: because of centralization. And a very *uneven* market: also because of centralization. Because in the crucial century between 1750 and 1850 the consequence of centralization is that in most European countries the majority of novels are, quite simply, *foreign books*. Hungarian, Italian, Danish, Greek readers familiarize themselves with the new form through French and English novels: and so, inevitably, French and English novels become *models to be imitated*. 'From the numerous national and local literatures there arises a world literature', reads the *Communist Manifesto*, but that's not how it is: rather, there arises a planetary reproduction of a couple of national literatures that find themselves in a peculiarly lucky position. 'One could amuse oneself', writes Pieter de Meijer, 'writing a history of the novel in Italy without mentioning Italian novels'.[44] 'There was a demand for foreign products, and production had to comply', adds Luca Toschi of the Italian narrative market around 1800.[45] A generation later, in Spain, 'readers are not interested in the originality of the Spanish novel; their only desire is that it would adhere to those foreign models with which they have become familiar': and so, concludes Elisa Martí-López, one may say that between 1800 and 1850 'the Spanish novel is being written in France'.[46]

Outside of Europe, the same power relations. For Edward Said, 'at some point writers in Arabic became aware of European novels and began to write works like them'.[47] 'One notices in Brazilian *feuilletons* what could be called a servile imitation of the French

---

[44] Pieter de Meijer, *La prosa narrativa moderna*, in Alberto Asor Rosa, ed., *Letteratura Italiana, Le forme del testo. II. La prosa*, Einaudi, Torino 1984, p. 762.

[45] Luca Toschi, 'Alle origini della narrativa di romanzo in Italia', in Massimo Saltafuso, ed., *Il viaggio del narrare*, La Giuntina, Firenze 1989, p. 19.

[46] Elisa Martí-López, 'La orfandad de la novela española: Política editorial y creación literaria a mediados del siglo XIX', *Bulletin Hispanique*, vol. 98, no. 2, 1995.

[47] Edward Said, *Beginnings*, 1975, Columbia University Press, 1985, p. 81.

90. The baroque crescent

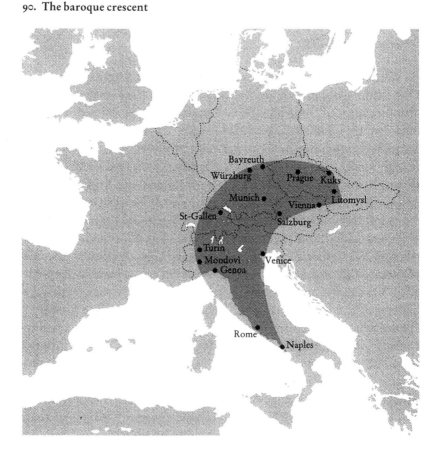

Let's open a map of Europe: baroque civilization takes form as a sort of crescent, with its south-western end-point in southern Italy, and the north-eastern one beyond Prague, and englobing Rome, Genoa, Turin, southern Switzerland, Venice, southern Germany, Austria, and Bohemia. The formation of this barrier of churches and monasteries can be explained with the necessity of countering the Reformation, and the austere commandments of Luther and Calvin, with a front of monuments pleasantly and richly decorated, such as may restore to the Catholic religion its lost appeal.

DOMINIQUE FERNANDEZ, *Le Banquet des anges*

91. The world of Cinderella

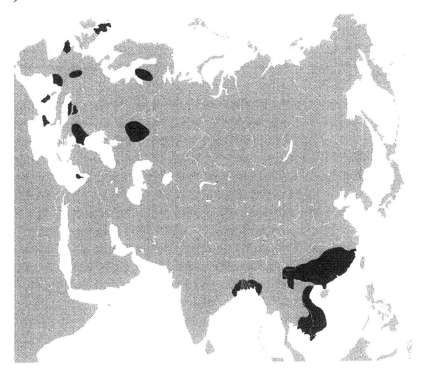

In the fairy tale of Cinderella [. . .] versions containing the gathering of the bones are documented in China, Vietnam, India, Russia, Bulgaria, Cyprus, Serbia, Dalmatia, Sicily, Sardinia, Provence, Brittany, Lorraine, Scotland, and Finland. So immense and varied a distribution precludes the possibility that the presence of this theme in the fable's plot is the result of a casual graft. A further hypothesis is permissible: namely, that the version which includes the resurrection of the killed animal is the more complete one.

CARLO GINZBURG, *Ecstasies*

model', writes Marlyse Meyer.[48] And Roberto Schwarz, in a formidable essay on 'The Importing of the Novel to Brazil':

> The novel existed in Brazil before there were any Brazilian novelists: so, when they appeared, it was natural that they should follow the European models, both good and bad, which had already become entrenched in our reading habits.[49]

It was natural, yes. 'It is intrinsically easier to borrow than to invent', writes William McNeill; and Torsten Hägerstrand: 'the human being is a satisficer, not an optimizer [. . .] To find just one workable solution is probably enough.'[50] And indeed, if Walter Scott's model works well in Britain – why not use it also in Spain, or Hungary, or Italy? It saves time and work (and a lot of blunders, probably). Here lie the deep, tenacious roots of diffusion: the great *conservative* factor in cultural history, as A.L. Kroeber has called it.[51] Which is true, and beautifully counterintuitive: because one looks, say, at the maps of *Don Quixote*'s translations, and sees movement, change: but underneath that change, Kroeber says, lies its opposite – the growing *sameness* of European literary taste.

Yes, once a 'satisfying' model is found, the history of a form becomes different indeed. Around 1750, at the time of the first rise of the novel, no such model exists yet, and the novel is as diverse, as free – as crazy, in fact, as could be: Satire and Tears, Picaresque and Philosophy, Travel, Pornography, Autobiography, Letters . . . But a hundred years later the Anglo-French paradigm is in place, and the second take-off is an entirely different story: third-person historical novels, and not much else. No morphological invention any more.

---

[48] 'O que è, ou quem foi *Sinclair das Ilhas?*', in *Revista do Instituto de Estudos Brasileiros*, no. 14, 1973, p. 46.

[49] Roberto Schwarz, 'The Importing of the Novel to Brazil and its Contradictions in the Work of Roberto Alencar', in *Misplaced Ideas*, Verso, London 1992, p. 41. And again: 'Foreign debt is as inevitable in Brazilian letters as in any other field, and is not simply an easily dispensable part of the work in which it appears, but a complex feature of it. It makes a significant contribution to our general body of culture . . .' (p. 50).

[50] McNeill, 'Diffusion in History', p. 76; Hägerstrand, 'Some Unexplored Problems', p. 221.

[51] 'Diffusionism', in Etzioni and Etzioni, eds, *Social Change*, p. 144.

Diffusion: the great conservative force. One form; and an imported one.

See here how geography is not a container, but a condition, and in fact a constraint of history – even of morphological history. Because, yes, we did know that France and England were the center of the European novel. But we had overlooked the consequences of this spatial pattern: the fact that – in an integrated market – latecomers don't follow the same road of their predecessors, only later: they follow a different, and *narrower*, road. They are *constrained* to it by the success of the products from the core: a veritable 'development of underdevelopment' in the literary field. Which is not a nice image, of course. But when you study the market, this is what you find.

9. *Theoretical interlude VI. Markets and forms*

Too pessimistic, what I have just said? 'The main idea I want to convey', wrote Gunnar Myrdal forty years ago,

> is that *the play of the forces in the market does not normally tend towards causing regional equality but, on the contrary, inequality.* 'Nothing succeeds like success', and I add: nothing fails like failure. The version in the Bible of this ancient folk wisdom is even more expressive: 'Unto everyone which hath shall be given and from him that has not, even that he hath shall be taken away from him'.[52]

Unto everyone which hath shall be given ... It's the terrible *solidity* of successful forms: the 'inflexible box' of Kuhn's paradigm, Gould and Eldredge's punctuated equilibria, Brian Arthur's increasing returns. Or to turn once more to the evolution of technology:

[52] Gunnar Myrdal, *Development and Under-development. A Note on the Mechanism of National and International Economic Inequality*, National Bank of Egypt, Cairo 1956, p. 27 (emphasis mine). And again: 'If things were left to the market forces without any policy interferences, industrial production, commerce, banking, insurance, shipping, and, indeed, almost every economic activity which in a developing economy tends to give a bigger than average return *and, in addition, science, art, literature, education and higher culture generally, would cluster to certain localities* and regions, leaving the rest of the country more or less in the backwater' (p. 28; emphasis mine).

After an early period of experimentation, automobile design stabilized by 1902 and did not change radically until 1959. In Kuhnian terms, a period of 'normal technology' was then followed by a technological revolution, the precursors of which had been developing in the 1920s. A new period of normal technology was entered in the 1960s. After 1900, only two basic types of automobiles have been mass-produced.[53]

Only two cars! But the ubiquity of imitation, Hugill dryly goes on, 'has been hidden by the competitive nature of automobile companies. No company wishes to admit that its basic design differs little from that of others.'[54] No company; and also no publisher, or novelist – or critic, for that matter. They all insist on the originality of their products, like so many car salesmen, and for the very same reason: to sell. Which is human, but cannot hide the growing sameness that holds sway within the literary field – just as everywhere else.

I have tried to quantify narrative diffusion; to analyze its spatial dispersion; to find theoretical models that may explain its rigidity. And yet, the process retains a somewhat enigmatic quality. Why did it all work so well – and how? Mind you, diffusion *has* worked, and in such depth as to appear almost natural; but it isn't natural at all. Novels shaped by British history, or the geography of Paris: how can Italian, Russian, Brazilian readers enjoy them? Because they are all caught up in the same world-historical whirlwind? True, true – but at such a level of abstraction as to be almost useless. And even so, another question remains: *how* does diffusion work? A Hungarian, a Brazilian novelist wants to write like Scott, or Balzac; excellent; but what about the *technical* side of the task? What should be kept, of the original model, and what should be changed?

What should be kept, what should be changed. In his analysis of a similar process – 'the reduction of diversity to unity' in early modern France – Robert Muchembled has found an elegant answer: cultural diffusion works, he says, by combining 'syntaxe savante, et vocabu-

---

[53] Peter J. Hugill, 'Technology Diffusion in the World Automobile Industry 1885–1985', in Hugill and Dickson, eds, *The Transfer and Transformation*, p. 110.
[54] Ibid., pp. 135–6.

laire populaire'.[55] Cultivated syntax, and popular lexicon; 'a European model, and a local setting', as Schwarz writes for Brazil.[56] The form comes from the center, and remains unchanging; while details are left free to vary from place to place. In the terms of this chapter (and simplifying somewhat): as the historical novel spreads through Europe and then through the world, its *plot* remains constant (and 'British') – while its *characters* change (and become 'local'). On the one hand, the *solidity* of symbolic hegemony (one unchanging form spreading across the globe); on the other, its *flexibility* (details, that change with each different place, make the form recognizable and appealing to each national audience).

Variable characters, but a constant plot. At bottom, it's the model of *The Morphology of the Folktale*, where for Propp – in Aarne's catalogue of 449 folktales – 'the names of the dramatis personae change (as well as their attributes) [but] *neither their actions nor their functions change*'.[57] And yet, this asymmetric relationship between a form and its variants is not without conceptual problems. Thus Lévi-Strauss, in his famous critique of Propp:

> To his great credit, Propp discovered that the content of tales is *permutable*, but he too often concluded that it is *arbitrary*, and this is the reason for the difficulties he encountered, since even permutations conform to rules.[58]

Even permutations conform to rules ... But if they do, then *some of them are bound to be impossible*: the concrete materials of a given culture may well clash with the imported model, bringing the entire process to the brink of collapse. Roberto Schwarz:

> Brazil was importing a model, whose involuntary effect was to raise the profile of [the hero's] ideas and extend their compass [. . .] *in a way which was at variance with Brazilian experience. Or, from a compositional point of view: in a way which did not include the secondary characters*, who were responsible for providing local colour, in the general structure of things.[59]

[55] Robert Muchembled, *Culture populaire et culture des élites dans la France moderne (XVe–XVIIIe siècle)*, Flammarion, Paris 1978, pp. 341–2.

[56] Schwarz, 'The Importing of the Novel to Brazil', p. 46.

[57] Propp, *The Morphology of the Folktale*, p. 20 (emphasis mine).

[58] Claude Lévi-Strauss, 'Reflections on a Work by Vladimir Propp', 1960, in *Structural Anthropology 2*, Penguin, Harmondsworth 1978, p. 135.

[59] Schwarz, 'The Importing of the Novel to Brazil', p. 55 (emphasis mine).

A model 'at variance' with concrete reality. 'Nothing is more Brazilian than this half-baked literature', adds Schwarz of Alencar's novels: where 'style and structure run at cross-purposes': and from this 'disagreement between the form and the material' follow the 'incongruity', 'dissonance', 'juxtaposition', 'compositional defects' of Brazilian novels.[60] Nor Brazilian only. 'One of the problems of the early [Indian] novelists', writes Meenakshi Mukerjee, 'was to reconcile two sets of values – one obtained by reading an alien literature and the other available in life.'[61] 'The raw material of Japanese social experience and the abstract formal patterns of Western novel construction cannot always be welded together seamlessly,' writes Fredric Jameson of Karatani Kojin's *Origins of Modern Japanese Literature*. For Masao Miyoshi, the modern Japanese novel had 'an impossible program'; while Karatani speaks of the 'paradoxical fusion of democratic thought and *kambungaku*', and states that 'all of Soseki's long novels are failures'.[62] Or to return to Europe, very close to and very far from its core:

> The most ancient literary modes in Ireland are heroic, romantic, fantastic; and the remoteness of such aristocratic forms from everyday life is no fit breeding ground for the novel.[63]

Problems contradictions paradoxes failures defects unfit breeding ground cross-purposes half-baked . . . Markets and forms, reads the title of this section; well, *this is how the market influences questions of form*. In the case of the less powerful literatures (which means: *almost all literatures*, inside and outside Europe) – in the case of these less powerful cultures, the success of the Anglo-French model on the international market implies an endless series of compromise formations; and fragile, unstable formations: impossible

[60] Ibid., pp. 65, 51, 43–6.

[61] Meenakshi Mukerjee, *Realism and Reality. The Novel and Society in India*, Oxford University Press, Delhi 1985, p. 7.

[62] Karatani Kojin, *Origins of Modern Japanese Literature*, Duke University Press, 1993, pp. 42, 184; Fredric Jameson, 'Foreword: In the Mirror of Alternate Modernities', ibid., p. xiii; Masao Miyoshi, *Accomplices of Silence. The Modern Japanese Novel*, California University Press, 1974, p. ix.

[63] Terry Eagleton, 'Form and Ideology in the Anglo-Irish Novel', in *Heathcliff and the Great Hunger*, Verso, London 1995, p. 149.

programs, failures, and all the rest. It is, again, the 'development of underdevelopment' within the literary field: where dependence appears – unfortunately – as the decisive force of cultural life. And one day, who knows, a literary criticism finally transformed into a *comparative historical morphology* may be able to rise to the challenge of this state of affairs, and recognize in the geographical variation and dispersal of forms the power of the center over an enormous periphery.

10. *'Sustained by its historical backwardness'*

And is this all? 'Half-baked' replicas of a few successful models all the world over? Almost always, yes. Almost. Another essay by Roberto Schwarz, 'Misplaced Ideas':

> In short, if we insist upon the extent to which slavery and favour twisted the ideas of the times, it is not in order to dismiss them, but to describe them qua twisted [. . .] They are recognizably Brazilian in their peculiar distortion. Hence [. . .] we are still left with that experience of incongruity which was our point of departure: the impression that Brazil gives of ill-assortedness – unmanageable contrasts, disproportions, nonsense, anachronisms, outrageous compromises . . . [64]

So far, it is the scenario we already know. But the dissonance between Brazilian reality and European ideas, Schwarz goes on, *estranged* those ideas; and so, for a bizarre twist of history,

> our national oddities became world-historical. Perhaps this is comparable to what happened in Russian literature. Faced with the latter, even the greatest novels of French realism seem naive. And why? In spite of their claim to universality, the psychology of rational egoism and the ethics of the Enlightenment appeared in the Russian empire as a 'foreign' ideology, and therefore a localized and relative one. Sustained by its historical backwardness, Russia forced the bourgeois novel to face a more complex reality. [65]

Sustained by its historical backwardness . . . The formulation is appropriately paradoxical, here. It is *extremely* unlikely for

[64] Schwarz, 'Misplaced Ideas', in *Misplaced Ideas*, p. 25.
[65] Ibid., p. 29.

backwardness to be a 'support': but if, for whatever strange reason, this unlikely conjunction occurs, the horizon does indeed open up. If an 'impossible program' succeeds – well, a paradigm shift cannot be far away. Not by chance, Schwarz mentions here the two major breakthroughs of modern narrative: the Russian novel of ideas (1860–90), and Latin American magic realism (1960–90).[66] And in both cases, *the new model is the product of a new space*: the semi-periphery of Europe, the semi-periphery of the world-system (just as, earlier on, the powerful paradigm of the historical novel had itself arisen in the semi-periphery of the United Kingdom). A new space encourages paradigm shifts, writes Peter Hugill, because it poses new problems – and so asks for new answers.[67] It forces writers to take chances, and to try unprecedented combinations: like the novel of ideas (the melodramatic pleasures of the *feuilleton*, plus the intensity of ideological struggle); or like magic realism: this oxymoron, this 'impossible program', indeed, that re-combined what centuries of European fiction had so successfully split.[68]

[66] Actually, Schwarz refers to Brazilian Modernism, which predates the 'boom' of Latin American fiction by a couple of generations. But paradigm shifts are often preceded by less successful precursors, that lay out the essential aspects of the new form, and I don't think I have betrayed Schwarz's point by rewording it as I have done.

[67] Hugill, 'Technology Diffusion', pp. 131 ff. According to Thomas Hägg (*The Novel in Antiquity*, 1980, California University Press, 1991, pp. 100 ff.), the technical inventiveness of Greek romances was powerfully encouraged by the geographical displacement of the Hellenistic period. The same point is made by Oswyn Murray, in the chapter on 'The Orientalizing Period' of *Early Greece* (The Harvester Press, Sussex 1980, p. 81): 'it is the meeting of two different artistic traditions which is more likely to have a revolutionary impact, partly in substituting a new set of conventions for the old, but also by at least partially freeing men's vision from the unconscious tyranny of inherited schemata.'

[68] Why did the paradigm shift occur in Russia and Latin America – but not in comparable circumstances (in Japan, Austria, the Arab countries, the United States)? Beautiful question, which however requires a truly new literary history: a comparative historical morphology along the lines, say, of Barrington Moore's *Social Origins of Democracy and Dictatorship*, or Perry Anderson's *Lineages of the Absolutist State*. In the meantime, we should at least remember two things. First, that success and failure are highly *contingent* results: given slightly different initial conditions – say, the opening of the narrative fabric to oral African-American forms – the United States *could* indeed have produced a major paradigm shift in the history of the novel in the mid nineteenth century. But those conditions did not materialize, and the paradigm did not change. On the other hand, second, paradigm shifts are extremely *rare* events, and therefore what needs to be explained is not really their absence in this or that country (*which is precisely what we should expect most of the time*), but rather their occurrence (which is highly unusual).

And then, see what else happened with novels of ideas and magic realism. The outcome of a new geographical space, these forms then produced *a new fictional space*: the European battle of ideas of Russian novels, the planetary non-contemporaneity of magic realism. And note: Europe, the world. In a hourglass-shaped pattern, the contracting universe of the first two chapters – from the utopias and intercontinental journeys of much eighteenth-century fiction, to the nation-state, and then the capital city – seems to have reversed its trend, expanding into narrative systems of ever increasing width.

A new space that gives rise to a new form – that gives rise to a new space. Literary geography.

Index of names and works